Soul Compass

Soul Compass

TRUSTING YOUR INTUITION AND THE WISDOM WITHIN

LORI DOUPÉ SHERIDAN

To request permission, contact the publisher at:
publisher@innerpeacepress.com

ISBN: 978-1-958150-50-4
Soul Compass: Trusting Your Intuition and the Wisdom Within

October 2025

Published by Inner Peace Press
Eau Claire, Wisconsin, USA
www.innerpeacepress.com

Dedication

To you, the reader: May you trust the wisdom of your soul and live with joy, embracing the path that is uniquely yours. Let your soul compass guide you toward a life of purpose, connection, and fulfillment. May your intuition be your guiding light, illuminating each step as you journey forward.

Table of Contents

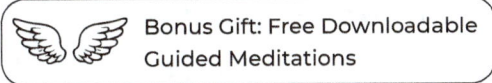 Bonus Gift: Free Downloadable
Guided Meditations

Acknowledgments

To my mom and dad, thank you for your unwavering love and support. Your encouragement has been invaluable, allowing me to express myself freely and pursue my dreams with authenticity. You taught me to trust my intuition and believe in the unseen. Though you are no longer physically here, Mom, I still feel your loving presence guiding me. I carry your love in my heart, always.

To my grandmother, thank you for your humor and steadfast belief in me. Your spirit continues to inspire me, reminding me of the importance of laughter, love, and kindness.

To my wonderful husband, thank you for your patience, understanding, and steady support. You are the rock of our family, and your quiet strength means more to me than words can express. I am truly grateful to share this journey with you.

To my beautiful sons, thank you for being my constant source of inspiration, love, and joy. You teach me every day about trust, wonder, and curiosity. Watching you both grow into young men with caring hearts fills me with a pride and love beyond what I could have imagined.

To my teachers, mentors, and friends – your belief in me has made all the difference. To my colleagues who inspire hope and uplift others through their work, thank you for reaffirming that love and life continue beyond the physical world.

Finally, my deepest gratitude goes to God, the angels, and all the unseen helpers who walk with us. Your unconditional love, wisdom, and grace have made this book a reality.

Foreword

$\mathcal{I}$ remember when Lori Doupé Sheridan first walked through the doors of the First Spiritualist Church of Quincy. It was 2006, and she immediately felt right at home, surrounded by like-minded souls who shared her deep curiosity and passion for Spirit. Even then, it was clear she was searching for something more, a deeper connection and a calling.

She quickly decided to begin her pursuit of spiritual knowledge, signing up for a class I was honored to teach. From the beginning, it was evident that Lori's skills were remarkable and simply needed fine-tuning. With dedication, heart, and a genuine love for Spirit, Lori worked hard to become the evidential psychic medium she is today.

I had the joy of watching her grow and develop, and like a proud Mama Hen, I was thrilled at each milestone she reached. Lori began to serve Spiritualist churches throughout New England and to further refine her abilities, she traveled to Arthur Findlay College in Stansted, England, a renowned place of study for mediums from around the world. During her time there, she fully embraced the opportunity to learn and deepen her connection with Spirit.

When Lori asked me if I would consider demonstrating with her, I was deeply honored and gave her a resounding yes. It has been a privilege to witness her journey firsthand and now to share the platform with her as a colleague. Our work together is joyous, bringing through loved ones from the Higher Side, giving them a voice, and sharing their messages of love, healing, and hope.

I am honored to call Lori both a dear friend and a respected colleague. I feel so blessed to have witnessed her growth and to see her blossom into the excellent medium and teacher she has become. She brings a rare combination of compassion, integrity, and heartfelt service to everything she does.

When Lori told me she was writing *Soul Compass: Trusting Your Intuition and the Wisdom Within*, I knew immediately it would be fabulous. This book is a true extension of her soul's work, offering readers encouragement, insight, and a loving reminder that intuition and Spirit are always within reach.

Lori is a blessing in the lives she's touched, and I know this book will touch many more.

Rita Berkowitz
Psychic Medium, Spirit Artist, and Author

Rita Berkowitz is an internationally recognized spirit artist, evidential medium, and ordained Spiritualist minister. She has taught and demonstrated spirit communication for over thirty years, including at the prestigious Arthur Findlay College in England. She is the author of *Empowering Your Life with Angels* and co-author of *The Complete Idiot's Guide to Communicating with Spirits*.

"Your soul knows the way. The key is learning to trust its quiet voice."
– L.J. Vanier

Introduction
Opening Your Psychic Toolbox

*I*f you're holding this book in your hands, know this: it's not by chance. This book found you for a reason.

Maybe you've been quietly wondering if there's more to life than meets the eye. Perhaps you've even felt a subtle nudge – an inner pull to explore your intuition, to trust your gut, or to understand the energy you feel around you. Or maybe you've had moments where you just knew something before it happened and have been waiting for someone to say: yes, that's real. You're not imagining it.

Whatever brought you here, trust that you were guided. You're exactly where you're meant to be.

This book is your invitation to explore the inner landscape of your soul. You're not starting from scratch – you're remembering something sacred, something that has always lived within you. You were born with intuition. We all were. Some call it a gut feeling. Others say it's a whisper from Spirit, or a knowing that rises from the heart. It's the quiet voice beneath the noise of everyday life – the steady compass pointing you toward truth, love, and purpose.

And like any compass, it works best when you learn how to read it.

You don't need to be a trained psychic or lifelong spiritual seeker to connect with your inner wisdom. What you do need is a willingness to slow down, pay attention, and trust yourself. Intuition isn't about predicting the future. It's about living fully in the present with awareness. It's a relationship, and like any meaningful connection, it deepens with practice, patience, and care.

This book is more than a guide – it's a sacred companion. It's here to help you reconnect with the wisdom you already carry and the voice of your soul that's been quietly guiding you all along. It's not about becoming someone new. It's about awakening who you've always been.

Let's take a moment to talk about the word "psychic." For many, it calls to mind a crystal ball, flickering candles, maybe a mysterious figure behind a velvet curtain. You might even picture Oda Mae Brown from the movie *Ghost* – the quirky, lovable medium who stumbles into her abilities and ends up transforming lives. That image might be entertaining, but it's far from the full picture.

Being psychic isn't about theatrics. It's about presence. It's about tuning into the subtle language of the soul and learning how to trust what you feel, sense, and know deep down. We're all connected – to each other, to

Spirit, and to something far greater than ourselves. And every single one of us has the ability to receive guidance from that connection.

You might be surprised to realize you're already doing this. Maybe you've known who was calling before the phone rang. Or had a strong urge to check on a loved one – only to find they needed to hear from you. Or perhaps you've simply walked into a space and sensed a mood before a word was spoken. These are not coincidences. They're glimpses of your intuition already at work.

Even if you don't fully trust it yet, that doesn't mean it's not working. The soul often speaks quietly – until we're ready to hear it more clearly.

As a professional psychic medium, I've spent years helping others recognize and trust these moments. I've shared in the joy of clients and students experiencing their own breakthroughs – those *aha* moments when they realize, *Wait, I felt that*, or *I knew that was going to happen*. Nothing brings me more joy than seeing someone reclaim their inner knowing and feel empowered by it.

Whether I'm teaching in workshops, giving a demonstration of mediumship, or sitting with someone in a private reading, my goal is always the same: to help people remember that they're not alone – and that their soul already holds the answers they seek.

We all have the key to this connection. Just like Dorothy in *The Wizard of Oz*, you've had the power all along. Sometimes, you just need someone to help you believe.

Throughout my own life, intuition has been a steady and trusted guide. One of the earlier moments I remember was sitting beside my now-husband on a moonlit beach during one of our first dates. The tide gently rolled in and out, and our conversation flowed just as easily – natural and effortless, like we'd known each other forever. I remember thinking, *This feels right*. My soul didn't shout. It simply whispered – and I listened. That moment anchored something in me: a quiet knowing that I was exactly where I was meant to be.

There have been deeper, more urgent moments too. The night before my husband's heart surgery, I lay awake, holding the weight of every fear. But just before I drifted off to sleep, something shifted. A wave of calm washed over me, and I heard it clearly: *He's going to be okay*. That simple message carried me through the surgery and gave me the strength to hold his hand in the ICU as he began to heal. It was my compass, once again, pointing me toward peace in the midst of uncertainty.

Motherhood, too, has sharpened my inner knowing. From sensing when to send a quick text to trusting the tug in my chest when something just felt off, my intuition has been a quiet but powerful force in how I care for my children. Once, during a family vacation, one of my sons got separated from the group during a bike ride. He had no phone, and every passing minute felt heavier. As my husband and I circled the neighborhood in our car, something inside me whispered, *Turn here*. And there he was – sitting calmly on a bench with his bike, waiting. Safe and sound. That moment reminded me that intuition isn't only about spiritual insight – it's rooted in love, connection, and instinct.

And then there are the sacred, soul-shifting moments – like the morning after my mother passed. The house was quiet, bathed in early light, and I sat in stillness, the ache of loss wrapping around me. And then I felt her. Not in memory, but in presence. Her voice rose within my heart: *We will get through this together. I will continue to hold your hand and walk with you. I love you.* In that moment, I knew – without question – that the soul continues, that love never dies, and that we are never truly alone.

These are the moments that matter. They affirm that our intuition is real. That we are always being guided. That we are part of something larger than ourselves.

This book is a reflection of that truth. It's a weaving of stories, tools, and insights gathered from my own journey and from the many people I've had the privilege to read for, mentor, and teach. Whether through mediumship, workshops, private sessions, or public demonstrations, I've witnessed countless ways Spirit speaks – and I've seen the joy that comes when someone realizes: *I can hear it too.*

And you can.

You'll find that intuition isn't just about tuning in to the spiritual – it's also about showing up more fully in your life. It's about navigating relationships, making choices that align with your values, and finding a sense of peace even when life is uncertain. You'll explore the psychic senses, learn how to notice signs and synchronicities, work with tools like pendulums, tarot, and meditation, and – most importantly – deepen your relationship with your own soul.

You'll also learn to recognize doubt for what it is: a natural part of learning. Especially when we're just beginning, it's easy to wonder, *Is this real? Am I making this up?* But with time, you'll learn to hear the difference between fear and intuition, between overthinking and true inner guidance.

Intuition is like a muscle – the more you use it, the stronger it becomes. Sometimes it whispers. Sometimes it nudges. And every once in a while, it roars. But it's always there, waiting for you to tune in.

Like any journey, the path of intuitive living isn't always linear. Some days you'll feel deeply connected. Other days, not so much. That's okay. Even when it feels quiet, your inner compass hasn't stopped working – it's simply waiting for you to pause, breathe, and return to center.

And if you ever feel uncertain, let this book be a touchstone. Come back to it as often as you need. There's no rush – just a remembering, a returning, a trusting.

And if you ever find yourself feeling lost, unsure, or off course, remember: even a compass needs to be held still for a moment before it can show you the way.

So, if you've ever longed for more clarity...

If you've ever wondered whether you're being guided...

If you've ever sensed there's more to this life than meets the eye...

This book is for you.

Each chapter is filled with stories, practices, and reflections designed to help you awaken your intuitive gifts and trust the guidance you've always carried within. Whether you're here to deepen your spiritual connection or simply to live with greater peace, this journey will meet you exactly where you are.

You don't have to walk it alone.

Take a breath. Let go of the noise. Open your heart.

The compass of your soul is already in your hands.

Now, all that's left is to follow where it leads.

"Our soul speaks to us in whispers, guiding us with a compass we carry within."
– Anonymous

Chapter 1
Awakening Your Psychic Senses

*H*ave you ever had a gut feeling that turned out to be right? Or sensed something about a situation before you had all the facts? These moments may feel like coincidences, but they're actually your inner knowing quietly guiding you – a gift we all carry within.

Intuition is your soul's natural way of communicating with you. It offers subtle insights, feelings, or impressions that lead you toward clarity and alignment. This wisdom is part of your eternal compass – something you already have. It's about learning to recognize the unique way you receive guidance and allowing yourself to trust it more deeply over time.

Psychic ability is an extension of that same inner wisdom. It's the ability to tune into energy, emotions, and subtle messages – both from within and from the world around you. You might sense what someone is feeling, see a mental image before something unfolds, or hear a quiet phrase in your mind that turns out to be important. These are all ways your soul may be guiding you through your intuitive senses.

Whether you're just beginning to notice these quiet nudges or have spent years developing your intuitive abilities, there is always room to grow. Your inner knowing is a quiet companion that can offer reassurance and guidance as you navigate everyday life. Like any relationship, it becomes stronger with practice, patience, and trust.

In this chapter, we'll explore how to awaken your psychic senses, recognize the ways your intuition speaks to you, and embrace the guidance that is already within reach. Trust that this journey is uniquely yours. With time and intention, your connection to your soul's wisdom will deepen and flourish.

Trusting Your Intuition: Real-Life Experiences

Our intuition often speaks in whispers, but its guidance can be life-changing when we choose to listen.

After my freshman year of college, I found myself feeling down and discouraged. I had been attending Northern Arizona University in Flagstaff and, despite earning straight As, I struggled to make friends. Shy and often nervous, I felt isolated and found myself driving home most weekends. Deep down, I knew if I stayed at this school, I might not finish college. I had to make a change.

That summer, I began researching colleges in Massachusetts. My mom's family was from the area, so I thought I might feel more connected there. I visited several schools, but none felt quite right – until I stepped onto the campus of Suffolk University. Nestled on historic Beacon Hill, with classrooms and dorms scattered around the Boston Common, the school immediately clicked. Something inside me said, *This is the one.*

Though nervous about transferring, I prayed, listened, and ultimately trusted the voice within urging me to go. That decision transformed my life. I thrived in Boston, making lifelong friends in my dorm suite and embracing opportunities I never imagined. My intuition had led me to a place where I could truly grow and flourish.

Graduating college marked a new chapter, but it wasn't long before one of my most profound intuitive moments emerged during a time of loss. On my way to visit my boyfriend – who is now my husband – I was suddenly overcome with a wave of nausea and dread. I couldn't explain it, but I knew something was wrong. When I reached him at work, I learned we had lost a close friend, Christian, in a tragic accident. Amid the heartbreak, this experience deepened my trust in intuition, reminding me that even in moments of loss, we are never truly alone.

Not long after, intuition guided me during a job interview. As I prepared, I felt an overwhelming sense of familiarity, as though I had already been to the office and lived the entire scenario. That deep knowing gave me confidence, and it became clear during the interview that this was where I was meant to be.

Years later, my husband and I were searching for a new home for our growing family. We walked into a beautiful yellow house that seemed perfect at first glance. Yet, as soon as we stepped inside, an uneasy energy lingered in the air. Without even discussing it initially, we both sensed something was off – it wasn't the right place for us. Trusting that gut feeling, we kept looking, eventually finding a home surrounded by nature and tall pines – a peaceful and quiet space that has been just right for our family.

One of my most impactful intuitive experiences came when deciding whether to attend a weekend mediumship development workshop with two teachers I deeply respected. As a mom, taking time away from my two boys was never easy, and the workshop stretched my budget. I hesitated, unsure if I could make it work. Then, I felt a sudden, undeniable message: *You're going. You have to go to this workshop.* The clarity was overwhelming. With my husband's full support, I registered and attended. That weekend not only deepened my abilities but also opened doors to opportunities and growth I couldn't have imagined.

These moments remind me that intuition is more than a subtle nudge – it's a profound force that connects us to the deeper knowledge of our soul. Listening to it allows us to access clarity, comfort, and guidance that shape our journey. By recognizing these subtle moments, we begin to see how intuition can profoundly impact our lives.

The Psychic Senses: A Sixth Sense in All Beings

Psychic abilities aren't unique to humans. Animals and nature also rely on remarkable instincts and sensitivity. A robin knows when to migrate, and a rabbit senses danger long before it arrives. Even our pets exhibit psychic tendencies.

Take my dog, Tasha, for example – a golden-brown shepherd mix with an uncanny ability to judge character. If she liked someone, she'd nudge them with her nose as if to say, "You're Tasha-approved." If she didn't, she'd give a low growl and keep her distance. Time and again, her instincts proved to match mine, offering a sense of comfort and reassurance that her judgments were often in alignment with my own.

Understanding the Psychic Senses

We all have access to what are commonly referred to as the psychic senses. These are ways we perceive information beyond our five physical senses. While we all have the ability to use each of these senses to varying degrees, most people naturally excel in one or two. With practice and time, each can be developed.

1. Clairsentience (Clear Feeling)

This is the ability to receive intuitive information through feelings. Have you ever walked into a room and sensed the energy without anyone saying a word? Or had a gut reaction about a person that turned out to be true? These are examples of clairsentience, where your feelings guide your perception.

How It Shows Up

For me, clairsentience often shows up as a feeling of comfort, ease, or emotional resonance – like your soul simply knows. When I meet someone I naturally connect with, I immediately notice how at home I feel. It's like a sense of warmth or familiarity, as if this person is sunshine for the soul. Years ago, while attending a retreat at the Omega Institute, I reconnected with someone I had known as an acquaintance. Over the course of the retreat, we spent more time together, shared laughter, and a deep sense of ease developed between us. That connection turned into a meaningful friendship – one that has offered mutual support through many of life's ups and downs.

Clairsentience isn't always about warm feelings, though. Sometimes it's the absence of comfort or a sense of unease that speaks just as loudly. I've learned to listen to both.

Exercise: Heart-Centered Body Scan

Purpose: To explore your clairsentience, or clear feeling, by tuning into your body and emotions. This practice helps you become more aware of your physical sensations and understand how your intuition speaks through your body.

Steps:

1. Find a quiet, comfortable space where you can sit without distractions. Close your eyes and take three slow, deep breaths to relax.

2. Bring your awareness to the top of your head and slowly move down your body. Notice any sensations, such as tension, relaxation, warmth, or coolness.

3. Continue scanning downward to your toes, taking time with each area. Focus especially on your chest and stomach. What emotions or sensations do you notice here? Are there strong feelings or gut reactions?

4. Reflect on your experience afterward. Write down any sensations that stood out, particularly areas of your body that seemed to "speak" to you more than others.

Notes

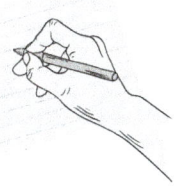

Throughout this book, you'll notice extra space after some exercises for your own reflections. Use these areas to capture insights, inspirations, and moments of personal growth along the way.

2. Clairvoyance (Clear Seeing)

Clairvoyance is seeing with your mind's eye, or what is commonly referred to as your third eye. When you close your eyes and picture a familiar place or visualize a symbol, you are using your clairvoyant abilities. This psychic sense often brings guidance through mental images, colors, symbols, or visions, though some people also experience external psychic visions. Once you begin tuning into your clairvoyance, you may start noticing images in nature – like angel wings in the branches of a tree or an abstract face hidden within a painting.

How It Shows Up

For me, there are many times I'll suddenly see the face of someone in my mind's eye – often unexpectedly – and then receive a phone call or text from them later that day, sometimes within minutes. These mental images arrive without trying, almost like a flash or a daydream, and they often turn out to be meaningful. I've learned to trust these visual nudges as my clairvoyance gently getting my attention.

Exercise: Imagery Practice for Clairvoyance

Purpose: To develop your clairvoyance, or clear seeing, by visualizing simple symbols and enhancing your ability to receive intuitive imagery.

Steps:

1. Find a comfortable space where you can relax. Close your eyes and take three deep breaths to settle your mind.

2. In your mind's eye, visualize a simple symbol – like a star, a tree, or an animal.

3. Hold this image and observe any colors, textures, or movements that arise.

4. If the image changes or other symbols appear, observe them without judgment. Reflect on how easy or challenging it was to hold the image and note any details that stood out. Write down your observations to track your progress.

3. Clairaudience (Clear Hearing)

Clairaudience involves receiving intuitive information through sound. This could manifest as a song popping into your head, only to hear it play on the radio moments later, or hearing a quiet internal voice guiding your choices. Clairaudience can be experienced both internally and externally (through seemingly external sounds or voices).

How It Shows Up

For me, clairaudience will often show up as a quiet phrase or thought that seems to come from beyond my own mind. It's not loud or dramatic – more like a gentle, inner voice that speaks with clarity and calm. I might hear something like, *Call them* or *Go now*, and later realize how meaningful that moment was. I've also had songs pop into my head with lyrics that provide comfort or insight, only to hear that exact song later that day. The key is listening without forcing – just noticing when something sounds like guidance, rather than a random thought.

Exercise: Silent Listening Practice

Purpose: To develop your clairaudience, or clear hearing, by practicing deep listening and noticing subtle guidance in the form of thoughts, phrases, or sounds.

Steps:

1. Find a quiet space free from distractions. Sit comfortably, close your eyes, and take three deep breaths to relax.

2. Start by focusing on any external sounds around you. Listen without trying to interpret or judge what you hear.

3. Gradually bring your focus inward. What do you hear? Are there any thoughts, words, or sounds that seem to come from within?

4. Allow these impressions to flow naturally, without forcing anything. Reflect on any thoughts, phrases, or sounds you noticed. Write down what stood out and how the experience made you feel.

The Core Clairs of Intuition

And one beautiful bonus you may experience through your dreams. Intuition speaks to each of us in unique ways. These "clairs" are the most commonly recognized ways intuitive messages can come through – sometimes as images, sounds, feelings, or even scents. You may naturally experience one or several. Trust that your intuition will develop in the ways that best support you.

⊛ **Clairvoyance (Clear Seeing)** – Receiving intuitive messages through images, visions, or symbols that appear in your mind's eye.
How to Develop: Practice visualization exercises and trust the spontaneous images that arise during meditation.

⊛ **Clairaudience (Clear Hearing)** – Perceiving sounds, words, or messages beyond the physical realm.
How to Develop: Spend time in quiet reflection, listening for subtle thoughts, words, or phrases that feel loving and encouraging.

⊛ **Clairsentience (Clear Feeling)** – Sensing emotions, energy, or physical sensations from people, places, or situations.
How to Develop: Tune into how you feel when you enter new environments or meet new people, noticing shifts in your mood or body.

⊛ **Claircognizance (Clear Knowing)** – Instantly "knowing" information without logical reasoning.
How to Develop: Journal intuitive insights without second-guessing – often, the first thought or knowing is the most accurate.

✹ **Clairalience (Clear Smelling)** – Receiving intuitive messages through scents, such as smelling flowers or smoke when none are physically present.
How to Develop: Notice any unexpected scents during meditation or prayer and what memories or impressions they evoke.

✹ **Clairgustance (Clear Tasting)** – Tasting something without physical contact, often associated with spiritual messages.
How to Develop: Pay attention to any unusual tastes during meditation or moments of deep thought, especially if they seem linked to a memory or loved one.

✹ **Clairtangency (Clear Touch) or Psychometry** – Receiving intuitive information by holding an object connected to a person, place, or event.
How to Develop: Practice holding objects (like jewelry or photographs) and notice any impressions, feelings, or images that come to mind.

✹ **Bonus: Clairvoyant Dreaming (Clear Dreaming)**
Receiving intuitive messages, guidance, or glimpses of future events through dreams.
How to Develop: Keep a dream journal by your bedside and record dreams upon waking – often, dream guidance reveals itself over time.

How Do You Most Naturally Receive Guidance?

Now that you've explored the core psychic senses, you may begin to notice how your own inner guidance already speaks to you. Some people feel things deeply. Others receive clear images, while some hear quiet words or phrases within. This section offers gentle prompts to help you reflect on how your soul naturally communicates.

There's no right or wrong way – only your way. Use the questions below to explore which psychic senses feel most familiar or consistent in your life.

Clairsentience (Clear Feeling):

- Do you often feel a gut reaction about people or situations?
- Have you ever felt physically uneasy in certain places or around specific people?
- Are you deeply moved by the emotions portrayed in movies or books?
- Do you tend to "just know" things about people without asking?

Clairvoyance (Clear Seeing):

- Do you clearly visualize things in your mind, such as places, people, or events?
- Have you ever had vivid dreams that seemed to predict the future?
- Are you drawn to colors, symbols, or imagery when seeking guidance?
- Do visual details stick with you more than sounds or feelings?

Clairaudience (Clear Hearing):

❀ Do you hear songs or phrases in your mind that seem meaningful?

❀ Have you ever known someone was calling you before you picked up the phone?

❀ Are you drawn to music or sound for comfort or guidance?

❀ Do you find yourself particularly sensitive to noise?

 **Exercise: Identifying Your Strongest Sense**

Purpose: To help you identify which psychic sense comes most naturally to you by reflecting on past experiences.

Steps:

1. Think about a time when you watched a movie. What captivated you the most? Was it the emotions and feelings of the story (clairsentience)? The visual aspects like the setting or costumes (clairvoyance)? Or the music and dialogue (clairaudience)?

2. Now, consider a visit to the beach. Did you focus on the sensation of the sand and water (clairsentience), the sight of the waves (clairvoyance), or the sound of the ocean (clairaudience)?

3. Reflect on these experiences and write down what stood out to you. Identify any recurring patterns in how you process the world around you and note which sense feels strongest to you.

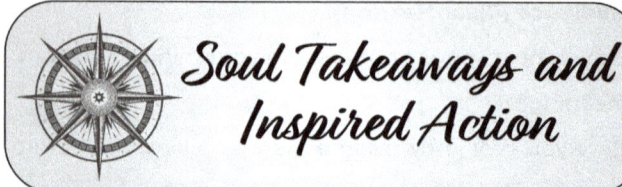

Soul Takeaways and Inspired Action

Your intuition is a compass that consistently points you toward your highest good. As you move forward, trust that you're not starting from scratch – you're remembering your way home.

Know that everyone has the potential to tap into their psychic abilities. By becoming more aware of your dominant intuitive senses, you can begin to strengthen and trust them – using them as a compass in your everyday life. Intuition is like a muscle: the more you use it, the stronger it becomes.

Begin by exploring which psychic senses feel most natural to you. Ask yourself: *Do I feel things deeply* (clairsentience)? *Do I visualize clearly* (clairvoyance)? *Do I hear that inner voice guiding me* (clairaudience)? Notice which of the clairs show up most consistently, and allow yourself to be curious. You can also begin to turn this into a fun and insightful practice. For example:

❋ Before answering your phone, pause and ask yourself: *Who might be calling?*

❋ Before entering a meeting or gathering, tune in. Can you sense who will be there? What the energy might feel like?

❋ Before heading home from work, pause and ask: *Which route should I take?* You might avoid heavy traffic – or something even more important.

✳️ Did a name or face pop into your mind, unprompted? If so, reach out. Often, you'll find they needed to hear from you in that moment.

✳️ Have you ever heard a phrase in your mind, like *Go now* or *Call them*, that didn't come from your thoughts but felt clear and distinct? That's often clairaudience – a subtle inner voice guiding you with love.

Keep a journal as you go. Note the intuitive nudges you followed – and the ones you didn't. Over time, you'll begin to recognize the difference between imagination and insight, fear and truth, coincidence and divine timing.

This journey is a lifelong unfolding. Be gentle and patient with yourself. There's no rush. The more you pay attention, the more you'll remember: you were born with this eternal compass. It has always been within you, quietly waiting to be heard.

Your soul knows the way. Trust that with each step, the path will become clearer, and the connection will grow stronger.

"You should sit in meditation for 20 minutes a day. Unless you're too busy, then you should sit for an hour."
– Zen Proverb

Chapter 2
Meditation: An Inward Journey

*H*ave you ever thought... "Meditation sounds great, but not in the middle of laundry piles, deadlines, or a noisy household." The truth is, meditation doesn't require a peaceful retreat nestled in the woods or a curated space with cushions, candles, or soft music playing in the background. It meets you exactly where you are – on the couch with your coffee, in your parked car between errands, or as you're lying in bed, eyes half-closed while the hum of the dishwasher plays in the background.

My own journey began with guided meditations I'd play before sleep. Some nights I stayed awake. Others, I drifted off mid-sentence. And that's okay. Just like intuition, meditation deepens with practice.

At its heart, meditation is about creating a small moment of stillness amid life's chaos, allowing you to connect with your intuition – the gentle whisper of your soul. Though in some traditions, meditation is taught as a path to bliss, it's not about emptying your mind or achieving perfection; it's about showing up for yourself, however that looks today.

When I meditate, it feels like hitting "pause" on the noise of life. Sometimes, it's waves of stillness and clarity washing over me; other times, it's a wrestling match with my to-do list. But no matter the experience, it leaves me feeling more aligned, more aware, and deeply connected to the wisdom within.

And the way you meditate doesn't have to be perfect. Meditation can happen while sitting quietly in your favorite chair with your eyes closed, or during a slow, mindful walk in nature. It could be lying in bed listening to a guided meditation, repeating a mantra, or simply taking a few deep breaths in your car before heading into work. Meditation is a personal practice – it's meant to meet you where you are. Whether you're sitting in stillness, driving in silence, or listening to music that soothes your soul, you're creating space for something sacred.

There is no one-size-fits-all approach. Meditation is deeply personal, and it's okay if it looks different from one day to the next. What matters is that you begin. Trust that with every breath, every pause, you're returning home to yourself. Your soul already knows the way.

Meditation is your soul's way of speaking to you, offering clarity and guidance that's always been there, waiting to be noticed. Let's explore how this simple practice can transform not just your day, but your life.

The Power of Meditation in Connecting to Your Soul

At its core, meditation is a journey inward – a way to connect with your soul, the essence of who you are. When we quiet the external noise and tune into the stillness, we create space for the soul to speak. This connection is a direct line to the intuitive guidance that exists within all of us.

When I began meditating, I often doubted the feelings or thoughts that surfaced. Was that really my intuition? Or just my mind playing tricks? But over time, I realized that this practice allowed me to tune into my inner knowing with more clarity. Meditation doesn't just calm the mind; it strengthens your ability to trust the wisdom of your soul.

My Meditation Journey

As my meditation practice evolved, I found myself moving from those initial guided sessions in bed to sitting in a special space in my home that I've come to call the "Zen Zone." It's a room with natural textures, pine beams, and large windows that allow light to flood in. Surrounded by towering pines outside, it feels like a sanctuary. I now sit here each morning, once I've gotten my boys off to school, and spend 15 to 30 minutes focusing on my breath. I connect not only with my soul but with something much larger – the divine, Source, God.

Some mornings, I feel waves of stillness and peace wash over me, and intuitive answers rise to the surface, quietly but unmistakably. Other days, my mind races, and I can barely stay focused, consumed by my to-do list. And that's okay. Meditation, like life, is an ebb and flow. Regardless of the experience, it allows me to feel connected – to myself and to the larger world around me.

On the days I miss my morning meditation, I find myself missing *me* – that quiet, grounding time I've come to treasure. It's become an important part of my daily rhythm, helping me feel centered, clear, and aligned. When I skip it, I often notice I feel a bit more scattered or less connected. In those moments, I gently pause, wherever I am, and take just a minute or two to focus on my breath and return to myself. Even the smallest act of presence is a way of saying, *I'm listening and honoring the wisdom of the soul.*

Meditation as a Tool for Intuitive Guidance

Just as our bodies need nourishment, so too do our souls. Meditation is a way of nurturing that inner self. Through this stillness, we become more in tune with the guidance that exists within. Our intuition becomes sharper, clearer, and more trustworthy. As we practice sitting in that quiet, we start to realize that the answers we've been seeking often come from within.

When I meditate, I don't just seek peace – I seek clarity. There have been countless times when I've asked a question and received guidance, not in the form of words but through a feeling or a knowing. It's as though my soul already knows the answer, and meditation creates the space for me to hear it.

Practical Tips for Starting a Meditation Practice

✺ **Find a Quiet Place and Time**: Consistency is key. It's helpful to choose a time each day when you can sit undisturbed. For me, that's the morning after my boys head off to school, but your time could be different. Whether it's five minutes or thirty, the regularity of your practice will help you create space for stillness.

✺ **Start Small**: You don't need to meditate for hours. Even just a few minutes of sitting quietly with your breath can have a profound impact. Many research studies have shown that meditating for as little as ten minutes a day can help reduce stress, improve focus, lower blood pressure, improve sleep, and enhance problem solving.

✺ **Set an Intention**: Before you begin, consider setting an intention. It could be to receive guidance, find peace, or simply to surrender to the moment. You may find that, with this focused intention, your meditation becomes a powerful tool for clarity and intuition.

✺ **Be Patient**: Meditation is a practice. Some days will feel effortless, while others might be filled with distraction. Be kind to yourself in the process. With time, you'll start to notice the benefits in your daily life and may even find yourself craving that quiet space.

✺ **Explore Tools**: There are many ways to meditate, and the key is finding what works for you. Try walking meditation, guided recordings, or simply sitting in silence. You might also choose to focus on a mantra – a word or phrase repeated softly in your mind to help steady your focus.

It could be something simple like "peace," "love," or "I am enough." Choose a word that feels comforting or inspiring – something you'd like to cultivate in your life. Over time, this gentle repetition can become an anchor, guiding you back to center whenever your thoughts begin to wander.

Exercise: Guided Meditation – An Inward Journey

Purpose: To center yourself, connect with your inner wisdom, and cultivate a sense of peace and alignment.

Find a comfortable spot to sit upright with your feet flat on the floor and your hands resting comfortably on your lap. Gently close your eyes, allowing your focus to center on your breath. As you inhale, feel the air entering your body, and as you exhale, release any tension or stress. Allow your breath to deepen naturally, noticing a sense of relaxation with each exhale.

Imagine yourself stepping onto a quiet, wooded path. Feel the earth steady beneath your feet as you walk, and notice the warm sunlight filtering gently through the trees. The scent of pine fills the air, calming and grounding you with each step, allowing any worries to gently fall away.

As you continue, you come to the edge of a tranquil river. You find a comfortable spot to sit along the riverbank, perhaps beneath a strong, ancient tree or upon a smooth rock, feeling the gentle support of the earth beneath you. In this quiet space, feel the energy of the earth rise gently up through your feet, filling you with a sense of calm and peace. With each breath, visualize the light of your soul expanding from within, radiating outward with warmth and openness, connecting with the light of nature, the universe, and Source itself.

As you sit with this presence, allow yourself to listen without expectation. Ask gently: *What does my soul wish to share with me?* or *What guidance is here for me today?* and trust that the answers will come, either now or in the gentle unfolding of the day ahead.

When you feel ready, bring your awareness back to your surroundings, noticing the chair beneath you and the weight of your body grounding you once more. Take a deep, centering breath, and when you're ready, open your eyes, feeling refreshed, connected, and aligned with your inner wisdom.

Free guided meditation
"Sanctuary of the Soul"
Download at:
LoriSheridanMedium.com/soulgift

Overcoming Common Challenges in Meditation

Meditation is simple in theory, but in practice, it can bring up challenges. Many of us struggle with distraction, discomfort, or self-doubt when we first begin. Here are some tips to help you overcome these common obstacles:

- **Distraction**: It's natural for the mind to wander. When you notice your thoughts drifting, gently bring your focus back to your breath or your chosen point of focus. Think of this as a practice in itself, as each redirection builds your mental discipline.

- **Physical Discomfort**: Find a comfortable posture that supports you without strain. You don't have to sit cross-legged on the floor; a supportive chair or a cushion can work well. Over time, your body will adapt, and the practice may even help reduce tension.

- **Self-Doubt**: Remember, there's no "right" way to meditate. Each experience is unique. Trust that whatever arises in your practice is valuable, and avoid judging your session as "good" or "bad." With time, you'll gain confidence in your ability to meditate.

The Role of Intuition in Meditation

As you deepen your meditation practice, you'll find that it becomes a gateway to stronger intuition. With each session, you strengthen the connection between your soul and the guidance that flows through you. Trust what arises – whether it's a feeling, a thought, a visual image, or even a simple knowing. These impressions are the voice of your soul, guiding you toward your highest good.

Journaling Your Meditation Experiences

One way to deepen your practice is to journal after each meditation session. Writing down what you felt, saw, or heard during meditation can help you track patterns, insights, and progress. This process allows you to capture the subtle ways your intuition is growing and the guidance you're receiving.

Your journal can be a place where you reflect on any impressions, emotions, or ideas that surfaced. Were there moments of clarity? Did a specific question or intention get answered? Journaling helps you build trust in the intuitive messages you receive, and over time, you'll start to notice themes and recurring symbols that are unique to your spiritual journey.

Tracking Your Progress

As you continue to meditate, you may also find it helpful to track your progress. You can record the length of your sessions, any breakthroughs you experienced, or simply how you felt after each practice. This can help you observe how your meditation practice evolves over time.

By making journaling and progress tracking a part of your routine, you create a tangible way to connect with the subtle shifts that occur within you. These practices help you cultivate self-awareness, and most importantly, they strengthen your trust in the guidance you receive through your meditation and intuition.

Soul Takeaways and Inspired Action

Remember, meditation is a powerful way to connect with your inner self and awaken your intuition. Even a few mindful moments can open the door to greater peace, clarity, and soulful alignment.

You don't have to meditate perfectly, and your practice doesn't need to look the same each day. What matters most is your willingness to begin. By carving out just a few quiet moments – whether in stillness or movement – you create space to reconnect with your soul.

Meditation invites deep listening. As you continue, you may begin to notice subtle shifts: a growing calm, clearer inner nudges, or intuitive insights arising throughout your day. These are signs that your soul is speaking – and you're learning how to listen.

This is a lifelong unfolding. Be patient and gentle with yourself. Some days will feel expansive; others, quieter. Trust that every effort you make is meaningful, and that Spirit will always meet you where you are.

For your next step, consider beginning a simple daily meditation. Keep a journal nearby to capture any impressions, thoughts, or intuitive feelings. Over time, you'll see how your soul has been gently guiding you all along.

Let your breath be your anchor. In the stillness, your soul will show you the way.

Timeless Wisdom

"What you seek is
seeking you."
– Rumi

The wisdom you seek through meditation has always been within you. Trust that through the practice of stillness, your intuition will grow, and the answers you need will reveal themselves when the time is right.

"Our bodies communicate to us clearly and specifically if we are willing to listen."
– Shakti Gawain

Chapter 3
Tuning In:
Listening to Your Body's Wisdom

*Y*our body is a wise and faithful guide, constantly communicating with you through subtle sensations, emotions, and physical cues. These messages are your intuition in action, offering a direct line to your inner truth. Yet, in our busy lives, we often overlook or dismiss these whispers from within.

Have you ever felt a flutter of excitement in your chest before taking a leap of faith or a tight knot in your stomach when something didn't feel quite right? These sensations are not random – they are your body's way of guiding you, helping you navigate decisions and situations with greater clarity.

In this chapter, we'll explore how to recognize and trust the messages your body is sending. By tuning in, you'll uncover a powerful source of intuitive guidance that is always available to you. Whether it's a sense of lightness when something aligns with your soul or a feeling of unease when it doesn't, your body holds a wealth of wisdom waiting to be heard.

I've learned firsthand how transformative it can be to trust your body's signals. From making life-changing decisions to navigating everyday moments, listening to my body's wisdom has been an anchor of strength and clarity. Together, let's discover how to deepen this connection and embrace your body as an essential part of your intuitive compass.

Trusting My Body's Guidance

Years ago, I faced a life-changing decision: whether or not to leave my secure 9-to-5 job, complete with healthcare benefits and a steady paycheck, to pursue my work as a psychic medium full-time. I had been building my practice for years as a side hustle, working nights and weekends, and dreamed of making it my primary focus. Yet, the financial responsibility of supporting my family loomed large. I found myself asking: *Will I be able to make enough money to meet my obligations?*

Every morning and night, I prayed for guidance: "God, if you're listening, please let me know if this leap is for my highest and best." I would meditate, set the intention for clarity, and quietly listen. But I wasn't just listening with my heart or mind – I started tuning into the signals from my body.

At first, I felt intense anxiety at the thought of giving up security. My stomach would tighten, and I'd feel nauseous whenever I considered the change. Over time, though, as I continued to meditate, pray, and sit in stillness, I realized these reactions weren't a stop sign – they were signals of fear and the unknown. Yet beneath that anxiety, there was also a growing sense of peace, a feeling that it was safe to move forward.

Gradually, I began to trust my body's wisdom. And when my husband's job offered family healthcare benefits, I felt the final nudge from within: *It's time to leap.* I quit my job, and a month later, I was working full-time as a psychic medium.

How Your Body Talks to You

Your body is constantly communicating with you – through sensations of ease or discomfort, relaxation or tension. These physical cues are one way your intuition speaks to you. Just as your mind offers thoughts or ideas, your body provides sensations that can help you discern the right path. Studies in psychology suggest that our "gut feelings" can be powerful indicators of stress and intuition, revealing subconscious insights about our choices and experiences.

- ✸ **Pay attention to physical reactions**: How does your body respond when you think about a particular decision or situation? Does it feel tight, uneasy, or heavy? Or does it feel light, calm, or expansive? These sensations can provide valuable insight.

- ✸ **Notice patterns**: Do certain feelings arise when you're around specific people or in particular environments? If your body consistently feels tense in one setting and relaxed in another, your intuition may be sending you a message.

- ✸ **First impressions matter**: Often, our initial gut reactions are the most accurate. If something feels off immediately, that's a signal worth paying attention to. Conversely, if you feel peace or excitement, your body may be affirming that this situation aligns with your soul.

Body Language and Intuition

Psychologists have studied how subtle body cues, like micro-expressions, can reveal subconscious feelings. Intuition can show up in subtle body language and micro-expressions. You might notice:

❋ **Body posture shifts**: Slumping shoulders, tightening jaws, or crossing arms can indicate discomfort or anxiety about a situation.

❋ **Changes in breath**: Are you holding your breath, breathing shallowly, or sighing frequently? This can signal tension or unease.

❋ **Body temperature or tingling sensations**: A sudden chill, warmth, goose bumps, or tingling can signal shifts in energy or alertness to a situation's meaning for you.

 **Exercise: Daily Body Check-In**

Purpose: To develop the habit of regularly tuning into your body's messages.

Steps:

1. Set aside a few moments each day, either in the morning or evening, to check in with your body.

2. Ask yourself: *How am I feeling right now? What sensations am I experiencing?* Pay attention to any areas of tightness, warmth, or relaxation.

3. Reflect on what you noticed. This practice can help you identify patterns and messages that your body is communicating.

Exercise: Body Awareness Meditation

Purpose: To connect with your intuition by paying close attention to the sensations in your body.

Find a quiet space where you won't be disturbed and sit comfortably with your feet flat on the floor or lie down if that feels better. Close your eyes and take a few deep breaths, allowing your body to relax. Slowly bring your awareness to each part of your body, starting with your feet and moving upward to your head. Notice any sensations – tightness, warmth, tingling, or relaxation – without judgment. Once you feel fully relaxed, bring to mind a decision or challenge you're facing. Pay attention to how your body responds. Do you feel tension, warmth, lightness, or discomfort? Afterward, take a moment to reflect on your experience and journal what your body revealed. Note any patterns or sensations that feel significant and revisit this practice whenever you seek intuitive clarity.

Exercise: Movement Meditation

Purpose: To deepen your connection to your body through movement, enhancing your intuitive awareness.

Choose a form of movement that feels natural to you, such as yoga, dancing, or gentle stretching. As you move, bring your awareness to the sensations in your muscles and joints, noticing how your body feels as you stretch, bend, or sway. Let your movements flow intuitively, guided by what feels comfortable and nurturing in the moment. Afterward, take time to reflect on how this practice helped you connect with your body's inner wisdom and heightened your intuitive awareness.

Exercise: Intuitive Eating Practice

Purpose: To become more attuned to your body's needs by focusing on the physical sensations that arise during eating.

Steps:

1. During meals, practice mindful eating by noticing how your body responds to different foods.

2. Pay close attention to the flavors, textures, and how your body feels as you eat.

3. Reflect on your experience. What foods felt nourishing? Did your body give you any signals or insights about its needs?

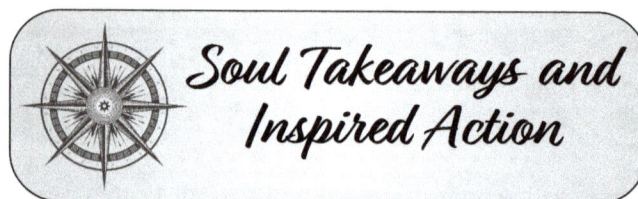

Soul Takeaways and Inspired Action

Take a moment to reflect on the messages your body has been sending you. Have you noticed those subtle whispers of intuition – the sensations that guide you as you navigate daily life? By honoring these signals and deepening your connection with your body, you empower your soul's compass to guide you with greater ease and clarity.

Begin by simply noticing how your body responds throughout your day. Do certain people, places, or choices make you feel energized or drained, calm or uneasy? These sensations aren't random – they're your soul's way of speaking through your physical self. They matter. They are the language of your inner wisdom made tangible.

Try checking in with your body regularly, especially during moments of decision-making. You might pause and ask: *Does this feel expansive or constricting? Is there tension in my chest, a flutter in my stomach, or a wave of calm?* These subtle cues are gentle guideposts, leading you closer to alignment.

As you continue to listen to your body's wisdom, consider journaling your experiences. What patterns emerge? What signals tend to show up when something is right – or when it's not? Tracking these impressions over time can deepen your trust in your body's unique intuitive language.

This relationship with your body is a lifelong unfolding. Be gentle with yourself as you learn its rhythms. With patience and presence, you'll come to see that your body is not only a vessel, but a sacred ally – a wise and loving partner on your spiritual path.

Remember: Your body is sacred. It holds the wisdom of your soul. And when you listen, it will always lead you home.

Timeless Wisdom

"To think is not enough – you must feel. Your body is the instrument of the soul."
– White Eagle

The soul often speaks through feeling. When you pause and tune in, your body becomes a master compass. Trust what you sense. Your soul is gently guiding you forward.

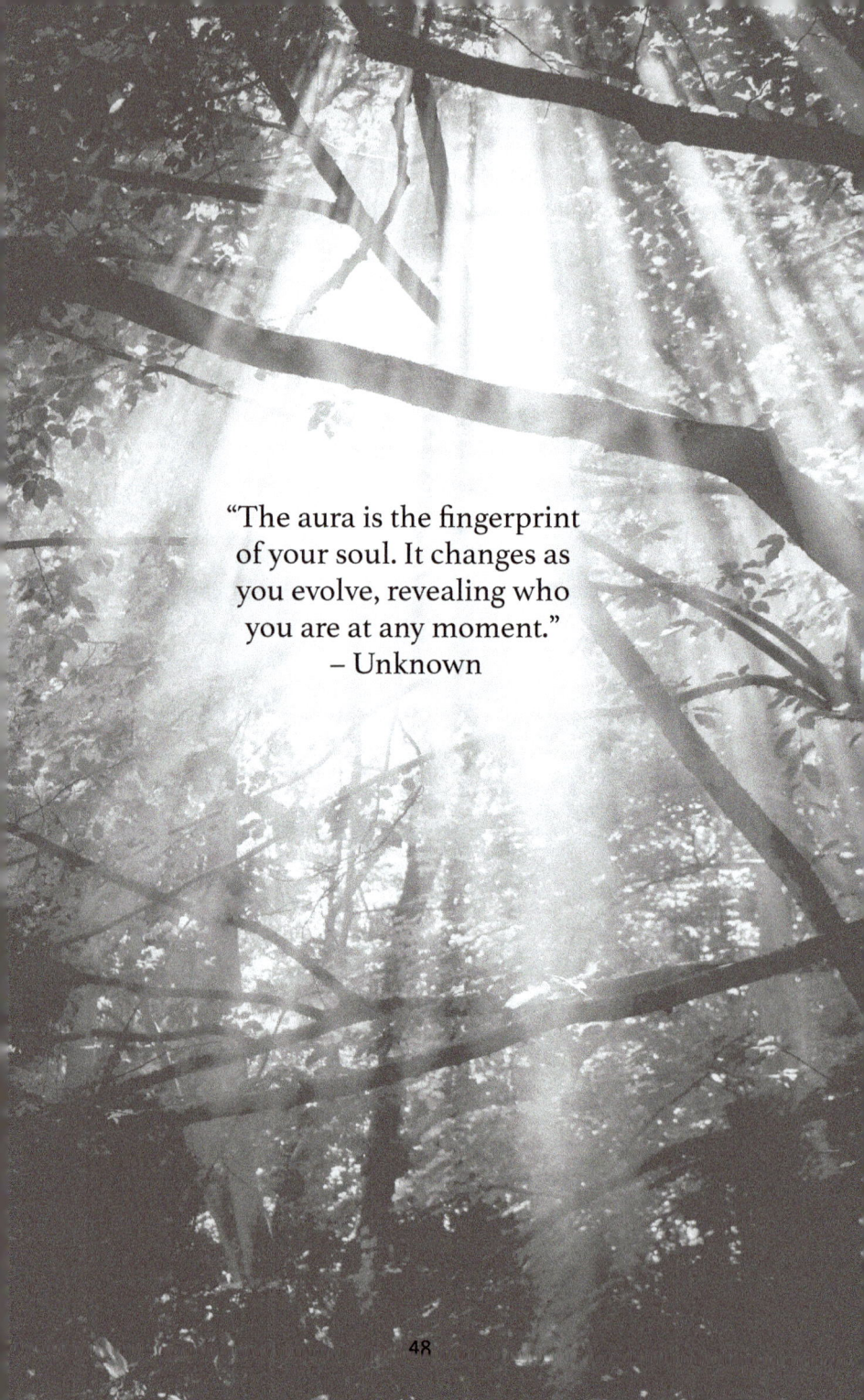

"The aura is the fingerprint
of your soul. It changes as
you evolve, revealing who
you are at any moment."
– Unknown

Chapter 4
Exploring Auras:
Understanding Energy and Color

When I first started exploring auras, I wasn't sure what to expect. Could I really see energy or colors around people? But surprisingly, with a little practice, it worked. My family members were kind enough to let me practice by tuning into their auras. We sat in the living room with natural light streaming through the windows, and I softened my gaze as I focused on their energy fields.

My mother's aura, a comforting green, reflected her nurturing nature as a nurse and therapist. My father's, a vibrant red after a workout, radiated vitality and strength. These early experiments showed me how intuitively our energy reflects who we are and how we feel in the moment. It also proved that sensing auras isn't just a mystical concept – it's something anyone can explore and develop with curiosity and practice.

Even if you've never noticed an aura before, you've probably felt someone's energy. Have you ever walked into a room and immediately sensed tension, even before anyone spoke? Or felt drawn to someone who seemed to radiate warmth and positivity? These are subtle ways we all perceive energy, whether we realize it or not.

Auras are part of this universal energy field, and learning to sense them can open a deeper understanding of yourself and others. In this chapter, we'll explore what auras are, how their colors carry meaning, and how you can begin to sense and interpret the energy fields around yourself and others. Whether you're looking to gain insight into your own emotional state or better understand others, exploring auras is a powerful step on your intuitive journey.

What is the Aura?

We are all surrounded by a vibrant energy field, often called the aura. With practice, you can tune into this energy field intuitively, sensing the colors that surround people, situations, and even yourself on a daily basis. These colors carry messages and insights, helping you to better understand both yourself and the world around you. Whether you physically see these colors or feel them intuitively, they are a powerful tool for personal awareness and insight.

The aura is an energy field that radiates from all living beings. It expands when we are relaxed and contracts when we feel anxious or threatened. While some people may see auras with their physical eyes, many find they can sense auras using their inner vision, mind's eye, or feel colors intuitively. You might have even heard someone described as feeling "true blue" or having a "warm, golden personality" – intuitively associating colors with certain qualities is a natural way we tap into aura energy.

Historically, colors have been linked to emotions and personality traits. Color psychology often shows how colors like red, blue, or green can influence mood and perception. Expressions like "green with envy" or "in the pink" reflect this intuitive association. Artists throughout history have incorporated this symbolism as well. During the Renaissance, artists often painted halos or radiant lights around figures like saints and angels, symbolizing spiritual energy or divinity. Perhaps these artists were capturing an essence of the aura, unconsciously depicting the energy that surrounds us all.

Our aura colors are not fixed; they can change depending on our mental, emotional, or spiritual state. This is why someone going through a joyful time may radiate bright, vibrant colors, while someone experiencing stress or emotional challenges might emit darker, muted shades. By tuning into these colors, you can gain insight into your current state or understand the emotions and energy of others.

The Colors and Their Meanings

Colors in the aura offer insights into emotional, spiritual, and physical states. While the following descriptions serve as a general guide based on my own experiences and studies, certain colors may hold unique meanings for you as well. As you explore your connection with colors, allow space for personal insights to emerge, trusting that your intuition may add layers of meaning to these interpretations.

- ✳ **Red**: Signifies vitality, strength, and passion. It's the color of action and leadership, often seen in those who are driven, determined, or highly energetic. However, red can also indicate challenges like anger or impatience, and it represents courage, love, and resilience.
- ✳ **Orange**: Embodies joy, creativity, and healing. It's often seen during times of change, symbolizing adaptability and an open heart. This warm color reflects vitality and compassion, encouraging personal and emotional growth.
- ✳ **Yellow**: Reflects intellect, logic, and curiosity. Individuals with yellow in their aura may be detail-oriented and focused on teaching or learning. Bright yellow represents creativity and mental clarity, while darker yellow shades may suggest stress or overthinking.
- ✳ **Green**: Associated with healing, compassion, and growth. Commonly seen in healthcare professionals or nature lovers, green reflects empathy, kindness, and a nurturing spirit. It also represents personal and professional growth, indicating new beginnings or transformations.
- ✳ **Blue**: The color of truth, communication, and emotional healing. It's seen in individuals who use language to inspire or guide, such as counselors or spiritual healers. Blue also reflects intuition and deep integrity, often seen in those connected to spiritual practices or creative fields.
- ✳ **Indigo**: Represents spiritual awareness, intuition, and imagination. People with indigo in their aura are often introspective and sensitive, possessing strong intuitive abilities.

Indigo suggests emotional depth and a journey of spiritual exploration.

- ❀ **Violet**: Violet signifies spirituality, intuition, and higher consciousness. Often seen in those devoted to personal or spiritual growth, it reflects wisdom, compassion, and a connection to the divine. Balanced violet energy suggests a deep sense of purpose and alignment with one's soul journey.
- ❀ **Turquoise**: Combines the compassion of green with the clarity of blue, symbolizing emotional balance, spiritual growth, and open communication. Often seen in those exploring their intuitive gifts or stepping into healing roles, it reflects a heart-centered approach to life and a growing connection with inner wisdom.
- ❀ **Pink**: Embodies love, compassion, and kindness. Often seen in caregivers or those with strong maternal instincts, pink reflects warmth, tenderness, and emotional healing.
- ❀ **Silver**: Suggests spiritual awakening, transformation, and divine support. This luminous color may appear during times of change or transition, indicating guidance from higher realms. It reflects an alignment with one's soul path and a heightened sensitivity to intuitive insight.
- ❀ **Gold**: Symbolizes wisdom gained through life experience. It's often seen in those who inspire others through hard-earned knowledge and inner strength. Gold represents enlightenment, resilience, and spiritual maturity.
- ❀ **Black**: Represents mystery, introspection, and potential. Black may appear during times of inner reflection or transition, representing unmanifested energy, waiting to emerge with clarity and purpose.
- ❀ **White**: Reflects purity, hope, and spiritual clarity. Often appearing during times of change, it suggests that new opportunities and spiritual growth are on the horizon.
- ❀ **Gray**: Often represents uncertainty, introspection, or stagnant energy. It can indicate that an individual is working through challenging emotions or decisions, preparing for greater clarity.

Exercises to Perceive Auras

Now that we've explored the meanings of different aura colors and how they reflect emotional and spiritual states, let's dive into some practical exercises to help you perceive and connect with auras more intuitively. Whether you're a beginner or have some experience, these practices will guide you in sensing the energy fields around yourself and others.

Exercise: Seeing Auras Objectively

Purpose: To begin perceiving auras visually by using a soft and relaxed gaze.

Steps:

1. Ask a friend or family member to sit against a neutral background.

2. Dim the lights slightly to create a gentle atmosphere.

3. Soften your gaze by relaxing your eyes and resting them gently on your volunteer rather than focusing sharply.

4. Observe the energy field around their head and shoulders. Allow colors or subtle shifts in the light to emerge naturally.

5. Trust the impressions you receive, even if they seem subtle or faint. Reflect on what you saw or sensed and write down your observations.

Exercise: Perceiving Auras Intuitively

Purpose: To sense the aura intuitively without needing to physically see it.

Steps:

1. Sit comfortably with a friend or loved one in a quiet space.

2. Close your eyes and take a few deep breaths to center yourself.

3. Ask yourself what colors come to mind when you think about their energy. Allow your impressions to surface naturally.

4. Trust your initial impressions, even if they seem subtle. Reflect on what you felt or sensed and note your observations.

Affirmation: Trust Your Senses

You are already sensing energy – whether through sight, feeling, knowing, or sound.
Trust that your experience is perfect for you.
The soul speaks in many beautiful languages.
There is no wrong way to see with the eyes of the soul.

Exercise: Interpreting Colors Around Situations

Purpose: To connect colors with the energy of situations or decisions for intuitive insights.

Steps:

1. In a meditative state, bring to mind a specific situation or decision.

2. Observe the colors you see or sense intuitively around the situation.

3. Reflect on what these colors might indicate about your feelings or potential outcomes. Write down your impressions to explore their meaning further.

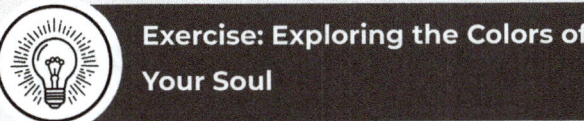

Exercise: Exploring the Colors of Your Soul

Purpose: To connect with your own aura and understand the colors you are radiating at different times.

Steps:

1. Sit comfortably in a quiet space where you won't be disturbed.

2. Close your eyes and take several deep breaths, allowing yourself to relax fully.

3. Ask yourself: *What colors am I radiating today*? Let the answer come intuitively without overthinking.

4. Reflect on the colors that come to mind and write down your observations. Consider how these colors might relate to your current state of mind or emotions.

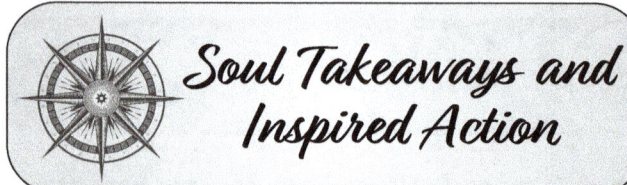

Soul Takeaways and Inspired Action

Exploring auras invites you to see yourself – and others – through the lens of energy and color. These subtle fields are living reflections of our emotions, thoughts, and spiritual essence in the present moment. They also extend around situations, environments, and choices, offering intuitive insight when we pause to notice and feel into them.

Begin by paying attention to how energy feels throughout your day. Notice the shifts when you enter a room or spend time with someone. Do you feel lighter, more open? Or perhaps drained, unsettled? These sensations offer valuable insight – they're your inner awareness responding to the world around you. You might also begin to sense the energy colors surrounding a person, place, or decision. Does it feel bright and expansive, or dull and clouded? These impressions can guide you toward greater clarity.

Take quiet moments to connect with your own energy. Ask yourself: *What colors am I radiating today?* or *What's the color of my energy right now?* Let the impressions come gently – there's no need to chase answers. Just notice what arises with curiosity and compassion. Similarly, when you're faced with a choice, you might ask: *What color is surrounding this option? How does it make me feel?* Sometimes a flash of color, a subtle shift in sensation, or a wave of feeling can offer more clarity than words ever could.

Try keeping a journal of your experiences with color and energy. Write down any impressions you have when tuning in to yourself, others, or situations. What colors appear during moments of peace or stress? What qualities do you associate with those colors? Over time, you may discover your own intuitive color language.

Remember, aura colors are fluid and ever-changing. They shift with your thoughts, emotions, and environment. Just as we grow and evolve, so too does our energetic field. This is not about perfection – it's about awareness and connection.

Allow this to be a creative and personal journey. The traditional meanings of colors can be a helpful starting point, but your intuition is the most important guide. Trust your impressions, even if they're subtle or surprising.

Be patient as you grow in this practice. Learning to sense auras is like learning a new language – one spoken in light, feeling, and energy. With time, it becomes more familiar, more natural, and deeply affirming.

You are not separate from the energy you perceive – you are part of it. The more you tune in, the more color becomes not just something you see or sense, but a trusted companion in navigating your day-to-day life.

"Synchronicity is an ever-present
reality for those who have eyes to see."
– Carl Jung

Chapter 5
Signs from the Universe:
Synchronicity and Guidance

—·†✳†·—

*H*ave you ever noticed how life seems to whisper to you at just the right moments? Perhaps a song on the radio answers a question you've been pondering, or you repeatedly see the same numbers wherever you go. These aren't mere coincidences – they're the universe's way of reaching out, weaving its guidance into the fabric of your daily life.

The universe speaks in a language of signs, symbols, and synchronicities. It's as if a loving friend is constantly leaving breadcrumbs along your path, gently reminding you that you are never alone. When we pause to pay attention, these messages not only guide us but also affirm that we are deeply connected to something greater than ourselves.

I remember a particularly challenging day when I had asked for a sign of reassurance. As I looked up into the sky, I saw a cloud clearly shaped like an angel. In that moment, I knew the universe was letting me know that everything was going to be okay – that things would get better. And they did, soon after. That simple yet profound sign filled me with hope and a renewed sense of trust.

In this chapter, we'll uncover the ways the universe communicates with us – from synchronistic encounters to the subtle nudges of intuition. Together, we'll explore how to recognize these messages, decode their meanings, and open our hearts to the endless support that surrounds us. By tuning in, you'll discover that life is always conspiring in your favor, guiding you toward your highest good.

Understanding Synchronicity and Divine Timing

Synchronicity is a principle of the universe, aligning events through more than just cause and effect. The term was popularized by Swiss psychiatrist Carl Jung in the 1950s, who described synchronicity as "the meaningful coincidence of events that seem related but are not explained by conventional mechanisms of causality." Jung believed these moments revealed an underlying connectedness between the inner and outer worlds – a reflection of a greater, unseen order.

Widely explored in both spiritual and psychological literature, these moments often guide us when we need them most. They are whispers from the universe, signs that we are in tune with life's flow and aligned with our soul's purpose.

This phenomenon, often referred to as divine timing in spiritual traditions, brings the right people and opportunities into our lives at the perfect moment. When we trust our intuition and follow our heart, our soul leads us to the right path – even if we don't always see the full picture right away.

Examples of Synchronicity

✺ Imagine you're contemplating a significant life change, like starting a new job. Suddenly, you keep encountering references to that job in conversations, social media posts, or articles. Each occurrence feels like a gentle reminder from the universe, affirming your path.

✺ You might be struggling with a decision when a friend casually mentions a book that perfectly aligns with your situation. This is the universe providing you with guidance when you most need it.

Learning to trust the flow of life makes everything feel as though it is unfolding exactly as it should. Imagine yourself as a leaf floating on a river, gently carried by the current. Instead of resisting, embrace the flow and open yourself to opportunities for love, joy, and fulfillment. With patience and trust, you'll see the synchronicities that confirm you're on the right track.

Messages in Everyday Life

The universe communicates with us constantly, offering signs and guidance in ways that are unique to each of us.

License Plates, Billboards, and Road Signs

One way the universe speaks to us is through words or symbols on license plates, billboards, or road markers. These little heavenly "hellos" often show up just when we need them.

For instance, one morning, I felt particularly overwhelmed by work. That day, while driving, I spotted a license plate that said "CHILL," an unmistakable message to relax. Another time, I was on my way to adopt a beagle from a shelter but felt unsure. That's when I saw a license plate reading "ANGEL," assuring me that this little pup was meant to be part of my family.

When you encounter a sign, take a moment to notice what you were thinking or seeking guidance on. If you're deliberating on whether to accept a job offer and pass a billboard that says, "JUST DO IT," it might be your answer!

It's natural to question whether signs are real or if you're just imagining them. When doubt creeps in, return to how the message made you feel. If it brought peace, clarity, or a sense of encouragement, trust that it was meant for you. The more you believe in the guidance, the more clearly you'll begin to receive it.

Numerology and Number Sequences

Numbers carry energy and often hold meaning in spiritual and metaphysical traditions. Repeating numbers or patterns, like 111 or 444, may appear as divine messages meant to guide or reassure us.

One of my favorite numbers to see is 444. To me, it's a comforting reminder that angels are near, offering their support and guidance. I often notice these numbers on receipts, clocks, or even license plates, and they always seem to show up when I need them most.

I think the angels even have a sense of humor sometimes! One day, while grabbing my usual iced French vanilla coffee at Dunkin' Donuts, I decided to ask over the drive-thru speaker if they had honey. The guy on the other end chuckled and replied, "Only me!" – a playful response that made me laugh. Then, when I pulled up to the window, he said in his strong Boston accent, "That'll be $4.44." I couldn't help but smile. In that moment, I felt like I was getting a wink from my angels, letting me know they were hanging out and everything was going to be alright.

It was one of those sweet, ordinary moments made extraordinary by the sense that Spirit was close by. These lighthearted signs are beautiful reminders that we are loved and supported – not just during times of uncertainty, but in the day-to-day rhythm of life. They're quiet affirmations that we are never alone – that Spirit is near, walking with us through it all.

When you notice a number sequence, take a moment to reflect on what's happening in your life. These gentle nudges often come as encouragement or quiet reminders that you are seen, supported, and guided. Trust that the universe – and perhaps your angels – are working behind the scenes with love and care.

Common Numbers and Their Meanings:

0: New beginnings; wholeness and potential.

1: Keep your thoughts positive; you're manifesting quickly.

2: Balance, harmony, and partnership.

3: Creativity, communication, and divine support.

4: Stability and foundation; angels are near.

5: Change is coming; be open to new experiences.

6: Focus on harmony at home and in relationships.

7: Spiritual awakening; inner wisdom is guiding you.

8: Abundance and success are on the way.

9: Completion of a cycle; prepare for something new.

11: Intuition and spiritual alignment.

22: Manifesting dreams into reality.

Sequences to Be Aware Of:

111: Your thoughts are manifesting quickly; stay positive.

222: Balance and harmony; trust the process.

333: Mind, body, and spirit are aligned; divine guidance is near.

444: Angels are surrounding you with protection and support.

555: Major changes are coming; embrace transformation.

666: Balance material and spiritual needs; refocus on positivity.

777: You're on the right path; spiritual blessings are on their way.

888: Financial abundance is coming.

999: A phase is ending; new beginnings await.

By noticing and interpreting these numbers, you open yourself to a deeper connection with the universe and its gentle guidance. The next time you see a repeating sequence, pause and consider its meaning – your angels may be closer than you think.

Nature's Signs and Animal Messengers

Nature serves as a profound messenger, offering signs through its creatures, rhythms, and patterns. When we pause and pay attention, these gentle signals reflect the energy we're moving through – or quietly guide us toward what's next.

The more we stay open, the more we begin to notice these sacred nudges. A butterfly that flutters near you, a hawk circling overhead, or a ladybug landing gently on your arm – these may seem small or random at first. But as you learn to trust your instincts and listen with your heart, these signs become meaningful reminders that you are supported, connected, and gently guided by something greater.

Here are a few of the signs I often see and what they mean to me:

- ✸ **Butterfly:** Transformation and personal growth. A sign that you are evolving and emerging into a new chapter.
- ✸ **Bumblebee:** Enjoy the sweetness of life. You're entering a time of busy productivity and sweet results.
- ✸ **Cardinal:** A loved one is near. A beautiful reminder from Spirit that blessings and love continue from the other side.
- ✸ **Deer:** Gentleness, grace, and good fortune. A reminder to move softly and trust that something beautiful is unfolding.

✵ **Dragonfly:** A reminder of joy and change. Often appears during transitions. Pay attention to color for added guidance.

✵ **Grasshopper:** A leap forward or breakthrough. Trust your instincts – the timing is right to take a bold next step.

✵ **Hawk:** Expanded vision, insight, and clarity. A call to rise above the noise and trust your higher perspective.

✵ **Ladybug:** A magical time of opportunity. Make a wish – blessings are near.

✵ **Owl:** Inner wisdom and truth. A sign that answers lie within and that you already know more than you think.

✵ **Rabbit:** Fertility, creativity, and quick movement. Trust your instincts – a new path may be emerging quickly.

✵ **Snake:** A time of change and transformation. You're shedding old ways and making room for something new.

✵ **Turkey:** Abundance, gratitude, and blessings. A symbol of harvest and the generous gifts of the universe.

✵ **Turtle:** Slow and steady progress. An encouragement to keep going; patience will pay off.

When these signs show up, pause and reflect. What were you thinking about or asking for guidance on when they appeared? These messengers can help affirm your intuition and bring clarity to your current path.

While the meanings above offer a starting point, your personal associations are just as important. The same symbol may hold different meanings for different people – so trust what each sign means to *you*. Keep a journal of the signs you notice, what they might mean, and how they make you feel. Over time, you'll begin to create your own intuitive language with the natural world.

These sacred whispers from nature are gentle reminders: you are supported, you are connected, and you are never walking alone.

Personal Story: A Stag's Message of Encouragement

During Covid I was preparing for an online mediumship demonstration to benefit local food banks. Feeling nervous about working on a new video platform, I sat in my office, unsure of how it would go. Just before I started, I looked out my window and saw a stag with antlers staring back at me. I couldn't believe my eyes. In that moment, I knew the Spirit world was with me, offering support. The event went beautifully, and I've never seen a stag in my yard since. Signs like these can offer profound reassurance. Take time to reflect on what the natural world is telling you.

Music as a Channel for Messages

Music often carries messages that resonate deeply with our emotions. A well-timed song can provide reassurance, guidance, or inspiration when we need it most. For instance, a friend once shared how she was following an ambulance carrying her unresponsive mother to the hospital. Feeling terrified, she suddenly heard Bob Marley's "Three Little Birds" play on the radio, with the line, "Don't worry about a thing, 'Cause every little thing is gonna be alright." That moment filled her with reassurance, and her mother soon recovered.

Asking the Universe for Signs

With practice, you can actively ask the universe for signs. Specify a symbol or number, and trust that it will show up in unexpected ways. Writing down your question or intention can also help clarify your request.

When we ask, the universe answers – and sometimes it has a little fun making sure we notice.

One morning on my way to work, I asked for a rose as a sign of confirmation. While riding the T (Boston's subway), I sat across from a woman wearing a dress covered in roses. When I got off the T and started walking through the Boston Public Garden, I found myself behind someone wearing a Rose Bowl hat. And as if the universe wanted to make sure I didn't miss the message, when I arrived at my office and turned on the radio, the very first song that played was by Guns N' Roses.

Three roses in three different ways – each one a personal, undeniable nudge from the universe, affirming my decision. It was a beautiful reminder that when we ask, the universe answers – often in ways more creative, playful, and surprising than we can imagine.

When you ask...
Trust that your sign is already on its way.
It may appear quickly – or after you've let go of expectation.
The universe loves to answer.
Stay open.
Stay curious.
The magic is in the noticing.

Exercises for Connecting with the Universe's Messages

As you begin practicing these exercises, remember that the universe's messages often arrive in ways we least expect. Whether it's a subtle nudge or a bold affirmation, every sign serves as a reminder that you are supported and guided.

Keep your eyes and heart open. This means looking beyond the obvious and tuning in to your inner awareness. Is there a symbol that catches your attention? A phrase that repeats? A feeling you just can't shake? These quiet cues are often how Spirit speaks.

If doubt arises, know that it's natural. But don't let it overshadow your intuition. The more you believe, the more you receive. Let go of the need to have all the answers at once and trust that the signs will appear in their perfect time. What feels like a whisper today may become a clear message tomorrow.

Embrace the process with curiosity and trust, knowing that each step strengthens your connection to the wisdom that's always available. Stay open. Stay curious. And most of all, trust the nudges. They're guiding you in the right direction.

Exercise: Asking for a Sign

Purpose: To practice asking the universe for a specific sign and learning to trust its guidance.

Steps:

1. Find a quiet space where you won't be disturbed for a few minutes. Sit comfortably and close your eyes.

2. Take several deep breaths, centering yourself and clearing your mind.

3. Set an intention by specifying a symbol or number you'd like to see as a sign. It could be anything meaningful to you – a rose, a feather, or a particular number sequence.

4. State your intention clearly, either aloud or in your mind. You might also choose to write it down, as writing can help anchor your intention and signal to the universe that you're open and ready to receive. A short letter or journal entry to the universe can be a beautiful way to clarify your heart's request.

5. Over the next few days, stay open to receiving this sign, whether in physical form or through a conversation, song, or other mediums. Reflect on when and how the sign shows up and what it means to you.

Exercise: Tracking Synchronicities

Purpose: To become more mindful of synchronicities and recognize patterns that connect to your questions or intentions.

Steps:

1. Carry a small notebook or use your phone to note meaningful coincidences throughout the week.

2. Record the date, what happened, and what you were thinking or feeling at the time.

3. Reflect on how these moments connect to your goals or questions. Consider what patterns emerge and how each synchronicity might be guiding you along your path.

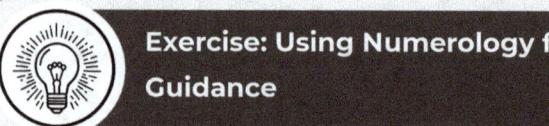

Exercise: Using Numerology for Guidance

Purpose: To explore how recurring numbers can provide insight and meaning in your life.

Steps:

1. Pay attention to any numbers you see repeatedly over the next week. These might be repeating sequences like 111, 222, or 444, or a consistent pattern of three numbers that keep appearing together, such as 318 or 527. Trust what catches your eye or feels significant.

2. Write down the numbers you notice and the context in which they appear, whether on receipts, clocks, license plates, or in conversation.

3. Reflect on the potential meanings behind these numbers and how they might relate to your current situation, emotions, or questions. What might the universe be showing you?

Exercise: Observing Nature for Signs

Purpose: To connect with the energy of the natural world by observing nature for symbolic messages.

Steps:

1. Spend time in nature, whether it's a park, forest, or even your backyard.

2. Notice any animals or natural events that catch your attention. Write down these observations and what you believe they might symbolize for you.

3. Reflect on these experiences and how they might be answering your questions or providing reassurance.

Soul Takeaways and Inspired Action

The universe is always speaking through signs, symbols, synchronicities, and subtle nudges that stir something deep within. When you begin to notice these messages, you enter into a dialogue with life itself. It's as though you've joined the quiet rhythm of a larger symphony, one that's been playing all along – and you are an essential part of it.

Nature, numbers, songs, and unexpected moments of insight often show up when we need encouragement or clarity. These are the gentle ways the universe taps you on the shoulder. Your role is simply to stay open, curious, and willing to listen.

It's natural to question or feel unsure at first. But over time, those quiet messages become more familiar, and your trust in them begins to grow. Meditation can help you tune in, and journaling what you notice gives the messages space to deepen and unfold. Even asking the universe for a sign can invite a more conscious connection with divine guidance.

Start by noticing the patterns that show up in your life. Does a particular number keep appearing? Are you drawn to a specific animal or symbol? These moments are invitations – breadcrumbs on your path – meant to guide you gently back to your soul.

The more you believe, the more you receive. You're learning to live in harmony with the signs around you and the wisdom within you. Every synchronicity is a reminder that you are supported, seen, and deeply loved.

Let the signs be your rhythm and your intuition the melody. You're already dancing with the universe. All you have to do is keep listening.

Timeless Wisdom

"Coincidence is God's way
of remaining anonymous."
– Albert Einstein

Synchronicity is the soul's way of getting your attention.
When you stay open and present, the universe responds
in gentle, unexpected ways. Every sign is a quiet
invitation to trust that you're on the right path.

"Dreams are today's answers
to tomorrow's questions."
– Edgar Cayce

Chapter 6
Dreams:
A Gateway to Your Intuition

—·✦ ✶ ✦·—

*H*ave you ever woken from a dream so vivid that it lingered in your mind for hours, as though it carried a message meant just for you? Dreams are like letters from our soul, offering guidance, clarity, and insight that our waking mind might overlook. Whether they are filled with symbolic imagery, flashes of the future, or the comforting presence of a loved one who has passed, dreams invite us to step beyond logic and listen to the language of intuition.

I've always found dreams to be a profound source of wisdom and reassurance. They have a way of bypassing the noise of everyday life, gently nudging us toward answers we may not have known we were seeking. Some of my most pivotal moments – decisions, realizations, and even connections with loved ones in spirit – have been sparked by the quiet yet powerful messages revealed in my dreams.

In this chapter, we'll explore the many ways dreams act as a bridge between the physical and spiritual realms. You'll discover the different types of dreams, their meanings, and practical tools to help you better understand their messages. Together, we'll unlock the potential of your dreams as a powerful ally on your journey to greater self-awareness, healing, and spiritual growth.

Dreams as a Gateway to Higher Realms

Edgar Cayce, often referred to as the "Sleeping Prophet," was a pioneering American mystic and spiritual teacher who lived from 1877 to 1945. Based in the United States, he gave thousands of intuitive readings while in a self-induced trance, offering insights on health, healing, past lives, and the soul's journey.

Cayce believed that dreams were sacred messages from the higher self and Spirit – a bridge between the conscious mind and divine wisdom. To him, dreams weren't random or meaningless; they were powerful tools for awakening, transformation, and guidance. He taught that through our dreams, we can receive answers to life's challenges, uncover our soul's purpose, and deepen our connection with the unseen realms.

His legacy continues to inspire spiritual seekers around the world to honor their inner wisdom and embrace dreams as a sacred channel for intuitive insight. Dreams offer a window into our subconscious, a mirror of the soul, and a compass for the journey ahead.

With this perspective in mind, let's explore the many ways dreams speak to us – each with its own rhythm, symbolism, and invitation to grow.

Types of Dreams and Their Meanings

Dreams come in many forms, each with unique characteristics and messages. Here are some common types:

Prophetic Dreams: When Dreams Come True

Prophetic dreams foretell future events, often through symbolic or direct messages. In these dreams, we may catch glimpses of upcoming experiences, relationships, or significant events in our lives. Prophetic dreams, noted for their accuracy in traditional and modern dream literature, can provide guidance when we need it most.

Personal Story: When I was pregnant with my oldest son, I had a vivid dream where he appeared to me, sharing that we would live together for a long time and that his name would be Kaiden. Later, I discovered that "Kaiden" comes from the Irish name Aodhán, meaning "little fire." Fittingly, he was born a month early under the Aries fire sign and has been a spirited teacher in my life, reminding me to stay present, live in the moment, and trust in the flow of life.

Symbolic Dreams: Messages from the Subconscious

Symbolic dreams communicate through imagery and metaphor, providing answers and guidance for life decisions and moments of uncertainty. These dreams help us tap into our subconscious mind's wisdom, often using symbols unique to each individual. Resources like dream dictionaries can help decode common symbols, though personal interpretations are always encouraged.

Personal Story: Before being ordained as a minister, I questioned whether this path was truly right for me, given the responsibility it carries and my sincere desire to help others through service. In a dream, I saw the Hamsa – a hand with an eye in its center – floating among the clouds. Curious, I later looked up the symbol's meaning and learned that it represents protection and blessings. The message was clear: I was on the right path, and it was safe for me to move forward with my ordination.

Anxiety Dreams: Reflections of Stress and Fear

Anxiety dreams often reflect our waking worries and insecurities, revealing the stress or unresolved emotions we may carry. Frequently recurring during times of heightened tension or significant life changes, these dreams may mirror common fears of failure, feeling unprepared, or being overwhelmed.

Personal Story: Even years after college, I sometimes have a recurring dream where I discover I've unknowingly missed an entire semester of a science class. I'm filled with panic, questioning if I'll be able to somehow pass the final exam and ultimately graduate on time. When I wake up, I'm relieved to realize it was just a dream, yet it always prompts me to reflect on any current stressors or challenges that might be triggering this old fear of being unprepared or inadequate.

Visitation Dreams: Connecting with Loved Ones

Visitation dreams are often the most vivid and emotionally charged, where we feel as if a loved one who has passed is truly present. These dreams, widely discussed in spiritual and psychological studies, offer comfort, support, and messages of reassurance.

> **Personal Story:** Shortly after my grandmother passed, I longed for a sign that she was still with me. Several months later, I had a dream where I found a pair of rose-colored sunglasses on a table. The moment I put them on, my grandmother appeared, smiling at me. The dream was so vivid and comforting that I knew it was more than just my imagination. I felt certain she was visiting to let me know that, even though I may not always see her with my physical eyes, she continues to watch over me from heaven.**

Other Common Dream Themes

In addition to prophetic, symbolic, anxiety, and visitation dreams, many of us experience recurring dream *themes* that carry their own intuitive messages. These dreams often speak to universal human experiences and emotions, offering insight into areas where we may be growing, healing, or feeling vulnerable.

** This story was first published in Alyson Gannon's book *Signs & Synchronicities: True Stories that Inspire and Empower,* published in 2024 by Franklin Rose Publishing.

Here are a few commonly reported dreams and what they might represent:

- ❀ **Flying:** A sense of freedom, spiritual elevation, or rising above limitations. It may suggest that you're gaining perspective or stepping into your power.
- ❀ **Running or being chased:** This can indicate avoidance, fear, or the pressure to confront something you've been putting off.
- ❀ **Drowning:** Often reflects emotional overwhelm or a sense of being "in over your head." It may signal a need to create more emotional balance or release pent-up feelings.
- ❀ **Public speaking or being unprepared:** A classic anxiety dream that speaks to fear of judgment, vulnerability, or performance pressure.
- ❀ **Teeth falling out or breaking:** Commonly tied to feelings of insecurity, fear of aging, loss of control, or communication challenges.
- ❀ **Romantic relationships or ex-partners:** These dreams often reflect unresolved feelings, lessons still integrating, or a symbolic exploration of self-worth and connection.

While these interpretations offer general guidance, your own associations are equally (if not more) important. A dream about flying might feel empowering to one person and unsettling to another. Pay attention to how the dream made you feel and what was happening in your life at the time. That's where the most meaningful insights live.

Enhancing Dream Recall

Whether our dreams are prophetic, symbolic, or simply an outlet for our worries, understanding them begins with recalling and recording them clearly. Dreams can be fleeting, but with practice, you can improve your ability to remember and reflect on them. Here are a few techniques to help enhance dream recall:

- ❀ **Set an Intention:** Before going to sleep, set the intention to remember your dreams or ask for specific guidance. Write your question or request on a piece of paper and place it under your pillow.

- ❀ **Keep a Dream Journal:** Place a notebook or recording device by your bed. The moment you wake up, jot down any details you recall, as they can fade quickly. Even fragments can carry valuable insights.

- ❀ **Make Time in the Morning:** Give yourself a few quiet minutes upon waking to reflect before jumping into the day. This small window can help you retain dream memories and capture them while they're still fresh.

- ❀ **Create a Relaxing Bedtime Routine:** Reducing mental chatter before bed can improve dream clarity. Try meditation, gentle stretches, or calming music to create a peaceful transition into the dream state.

Personal Story: Keeping a dream journal has been incredibly helpful for me. Personally, I use the talk-to-text feature on my phone when I wake up in the middle of the night. I quickly record my thoughts and email them to myself, ensuring I capture the details while they're still fresh.

Types of Dreams to Consider

Once we start remembering our dreams more vividly, it becomes easier to categorize and understand the types of messages they carry. Dreams offer guidance in many forms. Over time, you may notice themes in your dreams that help you discern their significance:

- ✷ **Problem-Solving Dreams:** These often reflect issues you're facing in your waking life, offering solutions or new perspectives. If you're grappling with a decision, set an intention for guidance and note any relevant symbols or actions in your dreams.

- ✷ **Recurring Dreams:** When a dream repeats, it may be urging you to address an unresolved issue. Reflect on the symbols, emotions, and patterns in recurring dreams to uncover messages that require your attention.

- ✷ **Lucid Dreams:** In a lucid dream, you become aware that you're dreaming and may even be able to influence the outcome. Lucid dreams are commonly explored in literature on dream work, offering tools for self-discovery, healing, and exploring the subconscious.

Lucid Dreaming Techniques

- ✷ **Reality Checks:** Perform reality checks periodically during the day by asking yourself: *Am I dreaming?* and examining your surroundings. This habit can train your mind to do the same while you're asleep, helping you recognize when you're in a dream.

- ✷ **Set Intentions:** Before sleeping, remind yourself that you want to recognize when you're dreaming and exert control within the dream.

Exercises for Engaging with Your Dreams

Each of these exercises offers an opportunity to deepen your relationship with your dreams, uncovering the wisdom and guidance they hold. As you explore the messages within your dreams, you may find that they illuminate answers to questions, provide clarity for challenges, or reveal profound truths about your journey. Now, let's consider how to integrate these insights into your waking life and continue building a connection with the divine guidance that dreams so generously provide.

Exercise: Reflect on Your Dreams

Purpose: To uncover the messages within your dreams and reflect on their meaning.

Steps:

1. Find a quiet place to sit comfortably with your journal.
2. Recall a significant dream that stands out in your memory. Was it prophetic, symbolic, anxiety-induced, or a visitation from a loved one?
3. Write down the details of the dream, including emotions, symbols, and any unique impressions.
4. Reflect on what the dream might have revealed. What personal or spiritual guidance do you think it holds?

Exercise: Dream Journaling

Purpose: To develop greater awareness of your dreams and identify recurring themes over time.

Steps:

1. Keep a journal or recording device by your bedside.
2. Each morning, record any dreams you remember as soon as you wake up. Include emotions, symbols, and key events.
3. Review your entries weekly to notice recurring themes or symbols. Reflect on what these patterns might mean in the context of your current life.

Exercise: Enhance Dream Recall with Meditation

Purpose: To improve your ability to remember and reflect on your dreams with clarity.

Before bed, take five minutes to meditate, allowing your mind to calm and your body to relax. Set a clear intention, such as: *I will wake up with vivid memories of my dreams.* Visualize yourself waking up and recalling your dreams in detail, feeling clear and focused. When you wake, take a moment to remain still and reflect on any dream fragments or impressions. Immediately record these details in your journal, noting any insights or patterns that emerge.

Exercise: Lucid Dreaming Practice

Purpose: To cultivate awareness within your dreams and gain the ability to influence their outcomes.

Steps:

1. Set an intention before bed to recognize when you're dreaming.

2. During the day, practice reality checks by asking yourself: *Am I dreaming?* and noticing your surroundings.

3. Track your progress in a journal. Write down any experiences with lucid dreaming and the insights they revealed.

Exercise: Recurring Dream Exploration

Purpose: To understand and interpret the messages within recurring dreams.

Steps:

1. Identify a recurring dream and record its key elements, such as symbols, emotions, and patterns.

2. Reflect on what this dream might be urging you to address or resolve in your waking life.

3. Write down insights or realizations that arise and consider how they connect to your personal growth or challenges.

Sample Dream Dictionary: A Personal Starting Point

As you begin tracking your dreams, you may notice certain symbols, people, or places appear again and again. These dream elements often carry meaning unique to you. While general interpretations are helpful, the most powerful insights come from your own intuitive knowing. Below is a sample of how I've come to interpret some of the symbols in my dreams – consider it a gentle guide as you begin to build your own.

- **Water:** Emotional depth, intuition, or spiritual cleansing. Calm water feels peaceful; rough water often reflects emotional overwhelm.

- **Bridges:** Transitions, moving from one phase of life to another. A clear, sturdy bridge often signals readiness; a broken one may reveal inner hesitations.

- **Birds:** Freedom, perspective, or divine messages. Whenever I dream of birds, especially soaring high, I take it as a reminder to trust my spiritual guidance.

- **Houses:** Different rooms often represent different aspects of the self. An attic might reflect old memories; a locked door might point to something I'm not ready to face yet.

- **Tigers:** Strength, protection, and fierce spiritual guardianship. I've had dreams of a tiger watching over my home – a powerful reminder that I'm supported and safe.

- **Spiders:** Creativity, patience, and weaving new possibilities. When I see a spider spinning a web, I often reflect on what I'm creating or envisioning in my waking life.

- **Car Accidents:** A loss of control or fear that something is veering off track. These dreams nudge me to slow down and reassess where I may be pushing too hard.

❀ **Climbing a Mountain:** A symbol of progress, persistence, and spiritual growth. Reaching the summit often feels like a moment of accomplishment – a reminder to pause and celebrate how far I've come.

These are just a few of the symbols I've worked with. Your list may look completely different – and that's exactly how it should be. Over time, you'll start to notice what symbols repeat, how they make you feel, and what they might be trying to tell you. Trust those impressions. Your dreams are speaking directly to you in a language your soul understands.

Your Turn

Begin your own dream dictionary here. Add symbols, images, and impressions from your dreams and note what they mean to you.

Soul Takeaways and Inspired Action

Dreams are one of the most intimate ways your soul speaks to you. They bypass the busyness of daily life and invite you to explore your inner landscape with curiosity and compassion. Whether they arrive as vivid visions or gentle fragments, each dream carries the potential for insight, healing, and intuitive connection.

You don't need to interpret every detail perfectly. Simply noticing your dreams, writing them down, and reflecting on how they made you feel is a powerful first step. With practice and patience, it becomes easier to recognize recurring themes, meaningful symbols, and intuitive nudges woven into your nighttime stories.

While dream dictionaries and outside sources can offer inspiration, trust your own impressions. The most meaningful interpretations are the ones that resonate with you personally. Your inner guidance is always present and uniquely attuned to your soul's journey.

Let go of the need to have all the answers right away. Believing in the value of your dreams invites greater clarity over time. You may be surprised by the wisdom that emerges when you hold space for reflection.

A dream journal can become a sacred mirror of your inner world – a place where patterns and personal symbolism begin to take shape. Each entry is a thread connecting you more deeply to your intuition.

The more you listen to your dreams, the more you'll come to understand their purpose. Even the simplest dream can hold a message just for you, offering comfort, guidance, or a gentle reminder that you are always being supported.

Timeless Wisdom

"Trust in dreams, for in them is
hidden the gate to eternity."
– Khalil Gibran

Dreams are more than stories of the night – they are soul-messages in disguise. Each one holds a key to your healing, your truth, and your connection to the divine. When you listen with your heart, your dreams become a sacred conversation with your higher self.

"Sacred tools awaken our inner knowing, inviting us to listen with the heart and act with trust."
– Unknown

Chapter 7
Sacred Tools for Intuitive Living

*H*ave you ever wished for a little extra guidance – a nudge from the universe to confirm you're on the right path? Sacred tools can act as just that, offering a tangible way to connect with your intuition and receive deeper insights. Think of them as bridges between your inner knowing and the practical wisdom you need for everyday decisions.

These tools aren't new. Many have been used for hundreds, even thousands of years, rooted in ancient traditions across cultures. From pendulums and tarot to runes and tea leaves, each carries its own lineage of sacred wisdom handed down through generations.

Whether you're new to these tools or have been working with them for years, this chapter offers something for everyone. If you're a beginner, you'll find simple and approachable ways to explore pendulums, tarot, and other intuitive practices. For those with more experience, I invite you to deepen your relationship with these tools, uncovering fresh insights and refining your practice. Sometimes, returning to the basics can bring surprising clarity or reveal something you hadn't noticed before.

These tools are accessible, empowering, and inspiring to explore. They don't replace your intuition; they amplify it – like adding color to a sketch or music to a quiet room. Along the way, I'll share personal stories, tips, and exercises to help you make the most of your practice and perhaps see these tools in a new light.

Let's begin with an open heart and a curious mind. No matter where you are on your journey, there's always more to discover. Together, we'll explore how to integrate these sacred tools into your life in a way that feels natural, empowering, and uniquely yours.

Setting an Intention: The Key to Working with Sacred Tools

Whenever you use a sacred tool, take a moment to set an intention. It can be something as simple as, "I seek clarity on this matter," or, "I am open to guidance for my highest good." This helps you focus your energy and lets your subconscious know that you're ready to welcome insight. Let go of attachment to the outcome, and trust what comes – even if it doesn't make immediate sense. Often, the clearest messages reveal themselves gently over time. With patience and practice, you'll begin to see how everything connects.

Pendulums: Tapping into Subconscious Wisdom

A Brief History

The pendulum has been used for centuries as a simple yet powerful tool. It's essentially a weighted object suspended from a string or chain, and it moves in response to energy or intuitive guidance. People have used pendulums for all kinds of things, from locating water underground to seeking answers to personal questions. It's especially great for yes/no questions, as it amplifies the subtle energy of your body to help reveal what you already know deep down.

Pendulums come in all shapes and sizes. Some are made of metal or wood, while others feature crystals that add their own unique energy. My favorite pendulum has an amethyst tip because I feel connected to its intuitive, spiritual energy. You might find one that just feels right to you – it might be the weight, the shape, or even the feeling you get when you hold it. The most important thing is that it resonates with you.

How to Use a Pendulum

Using a pendulum is simple and can be a beautiful way to tune into your intuition. Start by choosing a pendulum that feels good in your hand – it might be crystal, wood, or metal, suspended from a chain or cord.

Hold the top of the chain lightly between your thumb and forefinger. You may find it helpful to use your non-dominant hand, as it's often more neutral and less likely to influence the movement. Let your arm relax, keeping your elbow slightly lifted rather than resting on a surface. Sit upright and hold the pendulum so it dangles freely a few inches above your open palm or a flat surface.

Take a few slow, calming breaths before you begin. It's important to be patient – especially at first. If your pendulum seems slow to move, stay relaxed and give it time. Sometimes it needs a moment to respond to your energy.

When you're ready, ask the pendulum to show you a "yes" response. Observe how it begins to swing – it may move back and forth, side to side, or in a circular motion. Then ask it to show you a "no." You're simply getting to know its unique way of communicating with you. Some people also ask for a "maybe" or "not now" response.

Once you've established what each movement means, you can begin asking yes or no questions. These can be practical or personal – like "Is this the right time to move forward?" or "Would this food support my energy today?" Pendulums can help with clarity around daily choices, relationships, and spiritual growth.

Stay open and curious as you work with your pendulum. Like any intuitive tool, the more you engage with it, the stronger your connection becomes.

Personal Story: I often use my pendulum for day-to-day decisions. I remember when I was getting my first office space. I felt a mix of excitement and hesitation, wondering if it was the right step for my work. Before reaching for the pendulum, I paused and asked myself how it felt intuitively. Deep down, it felt like a yes, but I still wasn't sure. So I held my pendulum and asked, "Is this the right space for me?" It gave me a clear yes. That simple confirmation gave me the boost I needed to move forward, and the space turned out to be exactly what I needed.

Since then, my pendulum has helped me in many areas – from choosing venues for events to tuning into which foods feel most supportive. It has become a trusted companion, offering gentle validation for what I already sense within.

I've learned that it's always helpful to begin by checking in with your own inner knowing. What does your heart say? What feels aligned? Then, the pendulum – like many sacred tools – can serve as a way to confirm and strengthen the guidance you already carry inside.

If you're ready to explore the possibilities, here are three simple exercises to help you strengthen your connection and build confidence with this intuitive tool.

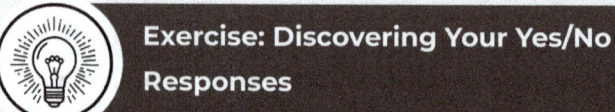

Exercise: Discovering Your Yes/No Responses

Purpose: To establish a clear understanding of how your pendulum responds to "yes" and "no," building confidence in interpreting its movements.

Steps:

1. Sit upright in a relaxed position. Hold your pendulum steady between your thumb and forefinger using your non-dominant hand, with your elbow slightly raised or supported so the pendulum can hang freely and still. Take a few calming breaths to center yourself.

2. Ask your pendulum, "Show me a Yes." Observe its movement – it may swing in a circle, back and forth, or in another direction. Just notice what feels consistent.

3. Next, ask, "Show me a No." Note how the movement changes. It might swing in the opposite direction or follow a different pattern altogether.

4. Practice by asking simple questions you already know the answers to, such as "Is my name [your name]?" or "Am I wearing a blue shirt?" Notice how your pendulum responds to each.

5. Once you feel more confident, try asking questions you're uncertain about. Stay open and relaxed, and observe the response without becoming too attached to a particular outcome.

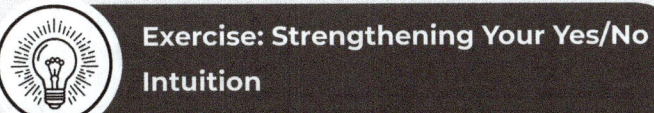

Exercise: Strengthening Your Yes/No Intuition

Purpose: To practice interpreting yes/no responses from your pendulum while remaining detached from the outcome, building confidence in your intuitive guidance.

Steps:

1. Create two cards labeled "Yes" and "No." Shuffle them and place them face down so the labels are hidden.

2. Quietly ask a yes/no question in your mind, focusing clearly on your intention.

3. Hold your pendulum over each card, observing its movement – whether it swings in a circle, back and forth, or remains still.

4. Which card did the pendulum show a "Yes" response to? That is your answer.

5. Flip the cards to reveal their labels, reflecting on whether the pendulum's response aligned with your question.

6. Practice with questions you know the answers to, gradually exploring questions where you seek guidance or clarity.

Exercise: Pendulum Hide and Seek

Purpose: To practice using your pendulum for locating hidden objects, enhancing your intuitive connection in a playful and practical way.

Steps:

1. Choose a small object, such as a ring or key. You can hide it yourself or ask someone else to hide it in a room for an added challenge.

2. Take a few deep breaths and center yourself. Quiet your mind and set a clear intention to locate the hidden object.

3. Hold your pendulum steady between your thumb and forefinger. Begin asking simple yes/no questions as you move around the room, such as, "Is the object in this area?" or "Should I look closer here?"

4. Pay close attention to how your pendulum responds. A "yes" may appear as a circular motion, while a "no" might swing side to side or remain still.

5. Continue to explore the room, following the pendulum's guidance and your own intuitive nudges to narrow your search.

6. Once you locate the object, take a moment to reflect. What sensations, movements, or impressions helped guide you?

Tarot: A Visual Language of the Soul

A Glimpse into Tarot

Tarot cards, which originated in 15th-century Europe as playing cards, are rich with symbols that reflect universal aspects of the human experience. A standard tarot deck includes 78 cards divided into two parts: the Major Arcana, which represents significant life themes, and the Minor Arcana, which explores day-to-day experiences.

The Minor Arcana is further divided into four suits – Cups (emotions), Wands (creativity and inspiration), Pentacles (the material world), and Swords (thoughts and the mind) – each offering insight into different areas of life.

A Brief History of Tarot

While tarot was first used for card games in 15th-century Europe, by the 18th century it began to take on a more spiritual and intuitive purpose. Over time, they became a sacred tool for reflection, insight, and inner guidance – rich with symbolism and archetypes that speak to universal human experiences.

One of the most well-known and influential decks in the modern era is the *Rider-Waite* tarot, created in 1909. Commissioned by scholar A.E. Waite, the deck was brought to life by artist Pamela Colman Smith, whose imaginative illustrations continue to inspire readers and artists alike. Her artwork helped make the cards more accessible and intuitive, paving the way for generations of spiritual seekers to connect with the wisdom of the tarot.

The Major Arcana: The Fool's Journey

The Fool's Journey, unique to the Major Arcana, symbolizes a path of personal growth and self-discovery. Beginning with the Fool, a card of innocence and potential, the journey moves through life's milestones, lessons, and triumphs. Each card represents a distinct phase of human experience, culminating in the World – a symbol of completion and fulfillment. This cyclical journey serves as a guide for exploring life's big questions, offering both depth and inspiration.

Personal Story: I had my first tarot reading nearly thirty years ago during a big life transition. The cards seemed to speak directly to me, validating feelings I hadn't been sure I could trust. Inspired, I bought my first deck – the Rider-Waite – and started learning the meanings behind each card. Some mornings, I draw a card to offer guidance for the day ahead or clarity on a specific situation. Each time, it feels like the universe offering me a gentle nudge to trust my intuition and stay aligned with my path.

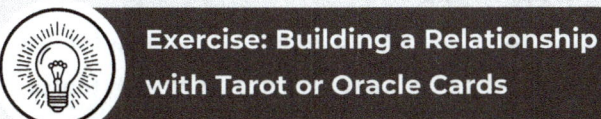

Exercise: Building a Relationship with Tarot or Oracle Cards

Purpose: To connect more deeply with your tarot or oracle cards by developing a sacred and consistent daily practice.

Steps:

1. Set aside time each morning to draw one card from your deck.

2. Study the imagery on the card and reflect on what it might mean for your day.

3. Write down your impressions in a journal, noting any feelings, insights, or recurring themes that arise.

4. At the end of the day, revisit your journal entry and reflect on how the card's meaning aligned with your experiences.

The 3-Card Spread

One of the simplest ways to use tarot is with a 3-card spread. You can use it to look at the Past, Present, and Future, or to explore a situation, advice, and the outcome. It's an easy way to get insight, and it's especially good for beginners.

Past	Present	Future
--	--	--
Situation	Advice	Outcome

The Celtic Cross Spread

The Celtic Cross is one of the most popular tarot spreads, offering a comprehensive view of a situation. With ten cards, it provides insights into the past, present, potential outcomes, challenges, and guidance. While the layout might seem intricate at first, it's designed to explore various angles of a question or situation with depth and care.

How to Use the Celtic Cross Spread:

Start by shuffling your deck and setting an intention or specific question for the reading. Lay out ten cards in the following positions:

1: The present situation

2: The challenge or opposing force

3: The foundation or root cause

4: The recent past

5: The possible outcome or future potential

6: The near future

7: How you see yourself or the situation

8: External influences or environment

9: Hopes and fears

10: The final outcome

Take your time to interpret each card in its position, reflecting on how the spread as a whole speaks to your question. Remember, the goal is to explore possibilities and gain clarity – not to predict rigid outcomes.

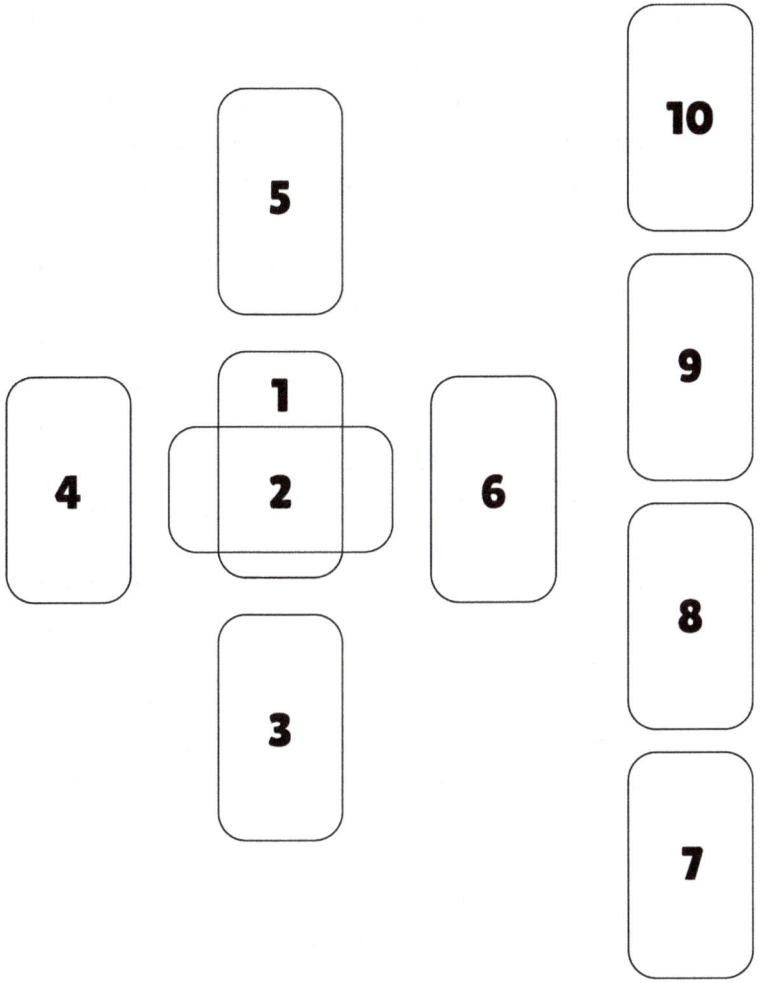

Psychometry: Reading the Energy of Objects

Psychometry is all about using touch to tune into the subtle energy held by physical objects. It's based on the idea that items absorb and carry the energy of their owner. By holding an object, you might be able to sense its history or the emotions connected to it.

Personal Story: In one of the first psychic mediumship development classes I took as a student, we practiced psychometry by working with personal objects. Each classmate placed an item in a bowl, and we were asked to intuitively choose one we felt drawn to. We didn't know who the objects belonged to, and we weren't given any feedback until after we wrote down the impressions we received. I was surprised by how much information came through – details about the person's personality and what was happening in their life at the time. It felt exciting and affirming to see how much we could perceive through the energy held in a single object.

In another class, we worked with objects that belonged to someone in spirit. Again, we were asked to hold the item and quietly tune in. As I focused, I picked up on the person's personality, how they may have used or worn the item, and their connection to the sitter. It was a powerful reminder of the deep emotional and energetic imprint we leave on the things we love.

We also experimented with a technique called billet reading. Each student wrote a personal question on a small piece of paper and folded it, with just a symbol on the front for identification. The billets were placed in a bowl, and we each selected one at random. Holding the paper in our hands, we tuned in psychically to any impressions that surfaced – without knowing the question or the person who had written it. Later, we found out whose billet we held and how the insights we received related to their question. It was amazing to witness how much could be picked up from such a simple object, and it deepened my respect for the quiet, sacred ways energy speaks.

You can try any of these approaches with a trusted friend or development circle. Whether it's a keepsake, a written note, or even something as simple as a keychain, you might be surprised by the stories and feelings woven into the objects around you.

How to Practice Psychometry

To try psychometry, choose an object that's special to someone – like a piece of jewelry or a favorite item. Hold it in your hands and relax, paying attention to any images, feelings, or thoughts that come up. At first, it might just feel like a vague sense or an emotion, but with practice, you'll start to recognize more details.

Ethical Considerations: Responsible and Respectful Use of Sacred Tools

As with many spiritual practices, ethical guidelines play a role in the responsible use of sacred tools, especially when interpreting information for others. Here are some essential guidelines:

❀ **Avoid Predicting Death or Diagnosing Illness**: It's best to leave these sensitive areas to licensed medical health professionals. Sacred tools are meant to uplift and guide, not diagnose or predict death.

❀ **Deliver Messages with Compassion**: Even if you sense challenging information, frame it in a way that respects the individual's feelings. Remember, everyone has free will and can choose their path.

❀ **Validate Rather than Direct**: Aim to offer options or insights rather than definitive answers. Empower the individual to make their own choices rather than telling them what to do.

❀ **Keep Information Confidential**: Protecting privacy builds trust. Never share details from a reading without explicit permission.

By following these guidelines, you honor the trust others place in you and the spirit of using sacred tools to uplift, inspire, and encourage.

Exploring Additional Sacred Tools

In this chapter, we've already explored the practical and insightful uses of pendulums, tarot, and psychometry – each offering a unique way to tap into your intuition. These foundational tools demonstrate how sacred practices can bring clarity to daily life. As we expand further, additional tools like oracle cards, runes, and tea leaves provide new opportunities to explore your intuitive connection. Whether you resonate with the structure of tarot or the free-flowing nature of oracle cards, each approach invites you to deepen your practice and uncover even more layers of guidance and self-awareness.

- ❋ **Astrology:** Astrology provides a detailed map of your personality, relationships, and life purpose through the study of your birth chart. By understanding the positions of the planets and stars at the time of your birth, you can uncover deeper truths about your strengths, challenges, and potential paths.

- ❋ **Scrying:** Scrying involves gazing into reflective surfaces, like a crystal ball, water, or a mirror, to receive intuitive imagery or impressions. The practice encourages relaxation and focus, helping you tune into subtle messages from your subconscious or higher self.

- ❋ **Divining Rods:** Divining rods, traditionally used to locate water, can also be used to find objects or areas of energetic significance. By holding the rods lightly and allowing them to respond to energy fields, you can uncover answers to practical or spiritual questions.

- ❋ **Palmistry:** Palmistry examines the lines, shapes, and features of your hands to reveal insights into your character and life path. The lines on your palms can reflect personal traits, potential challenges, and even spiritual growth opportunities.

- ❋ **Runes:** Runes are a set of ancient symbols often carved into stones or wood. Drawing runes during a reading can provide specific guidance and clarity, especially when exploring questions or challenges. Each rune carries its own energy and meaning, adding depth to your intuitive practice.

❋ **Oracle Cards:** Oracle cards, while similar to tarot, are more flexible and often centered around specific themes such as healing, self-discovery, or spiritual guidance. Unlike tarot, which follows a structured system with 78 cards, oracle decks vary widely in the number of cards and the approach to their meanings. These decks are ideal for those looking for intuitive insights without the detailed structure of tarot. By drawing a card and reflecting on its imagery and message, you can gain clarity and inspiration for your journey.

❋ **Tea Leaves:** Reading tea leaves involves interpreting the shapes and patterns left in the bottom of a teacup. This practice offers gentle guidance and insight into current circumstances or upcoming changes, helping you reflect on your journey.

By experimenting with these tools, you can discover new ways to connect with your intuition and receive guidance. Whether you prefer the structure of runes or the free-flowing insights of oracle cards, each method holds the potential to unlock a deeper understanding of yourself and the world around you. Each sacred tool is a doorway to your own soul's wisdom – patiently waiting to be explored.

Personal Story: Tea Leaf Reading

A friend once read my tea leaves, and I was amazed at how much she could tell about my life just by looking at the patterns left in the cup. She sensed things about my current challenges and even mentioned a sense of angelic guidance around me. It was such a simple but profound experience, reminding me how even the smallest things can carry powerful insights.

Exercises for Deeper Connection

These exercises are designed to deepen your connection with sacred tools and uncover fresh insights, no matter where you are on your journey. Whether you're just beginning or have years of experience, each practice offers an opportunity to refine your intuition, explore new perspectives, and strengthen your trust in the guidance these tools provide. Let's dive in and see where your inner wisdom leads.

 **Exercise: Creating a Custom Tarot Spread**

Purpose: To design a spread tailored to your unique questions, allowing for deeper insight and personal connection.

Steps:

1. Identify a specific topic or question you'd like guidance on (e.g., career, relationships, or personal growth).

2. Create a spread with three to five positions, each representing a different aspect of your question (e.g., Situation, Advice, Outcome).

3. Draw the cards and study their placement and meanings in relation to your question.

4. Write down your observations and reflect on how the spread's messages resonate with you.

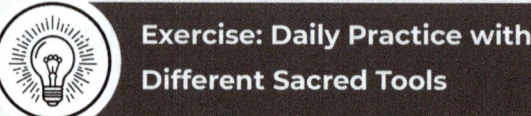

Exercise: Daily Practice with Different Sacred Tools

Purpose: To explore various tools and identify which ones resonate most with your intuitive style.

Steps:

1. Choose a different tool each day – pendulums, tarot, scrying, runes, etc. – and set aside 10-15 minutes to work with it.

2. Follow any relevant steps for using the tool and observe your experiences.

3. Record your impressions in a journal, noting which tools felt most natural or provided the clearest insights.

4. At the end of the week, reflect on your experiences and consider which tools you'd like to explore further.

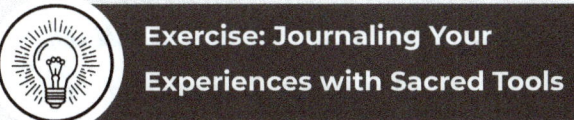

Exercise: Journaling Your Experiences with Sacred Tools

Purpose: To track your journey with sacred tools and identify patterns or themes in your intuitive practice.

Steps:

1. Set aside time each day or week to write about your experiences with sacred tools.

2. Record the questions you asked, the impressions you received, and how they related to your daily life.

3. Note any patterns or recurring symbols that emerge, reflecting on their significance.

4. Use your journal as a resource to deepen your understanding and confidence in your intuitive abilities.

Soul Takeaways and Inspired Action

Sacred tools are doorways to deeper understanding. They don't replace your inner voice; they simply help you hear it more clearly. Every time you reach for a pendulum, draw a tarot card, or hold a meaningful object, you're strengthening the connection between your conscious mind and the quiet wisdom of your soul.

The true gift of these tools isn't about predicting the future. It's about becoming more empowered to make choices that feel aligned in the present moment. With each use, they remind you to pause, reflect, and trust what's already stirring within.

Begin each practice with a clear intention. A quiet mind and open heart allow for more meaningful insights to rise to the surface. As messages come through – whether subtle or unexpected – acknowledge them with curiosity. Even gentle impressions can carry deep truth.

These tools work best as mirrors of the soul, not maps. They reflect your inner landscape and can offer helpful validation when you're navigating uncertainty. Over time, you may notice patterns, develop your own intuitive language, and feel more confident in your ability to receive guidance.

Journaling your experiences can deepen your practice. Writing down your impressions helps you track growth, recognize themes, and better understand the ways your intuition speaks to you.

When used with patience, intention, and trust, they become quiet allies – offering clarity, encouragement, and gentle confirmation as you move through life with greater awareness.

"Angels walk with us, not
as distant guardians, but
as friends, guiding us with
gentle whispers and the
unwavering light of love."
– Anonymous

Chapter 8
Meeting Your Spiritual Support Team

*I*magine that, from the moment you took your first breath, you were surrounded by a loving team whose sole purpose was to guide, protect, and encourage you throughout your life. This isn't a fantasy – each of us has a dedicated Spiritual Support Team on the other side, always there, offering love and wisdom through every high and low.

Whether you call them spirit guides, guardian angels, or just "your team," these loving presences are constantly working behind the scenes, ready to help whenever you reach out. Their love is unconditional, and their purpose is to support you in your journey of becoming the best version of yourself.

Perhaps you've felt their presence at pivotal moments – a comforting nudge to go a certain direction, an unexpected sense of peace when facing something challenging, or even a sudden idea that seemed to come out of nowhere. These are the gentle ways our guides remind us that we are never alone, and that they are always by our side, helping us navigate life's twists and turns.

In this chapter, we'll explore who these guides are, the unique roles they play, and how you can build a meaningful connection with them. You'll discover that communication with your spiritual team is not only possible but also incredibly rewarding, offering guidance that aligns with your soul's purpose and opens you to a life filled with more meaning, love, and synchronicity.

Free Will and Subtle Guidance

Many intuitive teachings propose that our guides honor our ability to make our own choices, rarely intervening without our permission. Rather than making decisions for us, they may communicate through gentle nudges, intuitive insights, or feelings. This kind of guidance supports our personal growth while respecting our autonomy.

> **For example:** You may feel an unexpected urge to avoid a particular path, only to later discover that something significant happened there. It may have been your guides gently steering you toward a safer route.

However, there are moments when your spiritual team may intervene more directly. In critical situations – such as life-threatening circumstances or major crossroads – they might take stronger action to ensure you remain on your soul's path.

Divine Intervention in Action

One of my friends had a profound experience that illustrates the compassionate guidance of our spiritual team. She was in an abusive relationship and felt trapped, unsure of how to leave and protect herself and her children. One night, as she lay awake in bed, an angel appeared at the foot of her bed, delivering a clear message: her path forward would be guided, and she and her children would be led to safety. The message gave her the courage to make life-changing decisions, and today, she and her children are safe and thriving. This powerful intervention shows how, in our darkest moments, we are never alone; our spiritual team is with us, offering hope and direction.

The Members of Your Spiritual Support Team

- ✳ **Spirit Guides:** Spirit guides are often described as mentors who offer wisdom, having possibly lived human lives and mastered specific areas of knowledge. Certain spiritual traditions suggest that guides bring tailored insights to each stage of life, offering guidance that aligns with our needs and personal growth.

- ✳ **Ascended Masters:** Ascended Masters, such as Jesus, Mother Mary, Kuan Yin, and others, are thought to be highly evolved spiritual beings. These masters, associated with universal principles like compassion and courage, are accessible to those who seek their wisdom and are seen as guiding humanity as a whole.

❀ **Guardian Angels:** Guardian angels are described in many belief systems as compassionate beings who accompany us from birth, providing unwavering love and support. Since they have not lived human lives, their energy is often considered especially pure and gentle.

❀ **Archangels:** Archangels are seen as powerful guides who can work with many people simultaneously, each specializing in an area of life. For example:

    ❊ **Archangel Michael:** Protector and bringer of courage.

    ❊ **Archangel Gabriel:** A messenger and guide for communication and family.

    ❊ **Archangel Raphael:** Healer for emotional, physical, and spiritual ailments.

❀ **Departed Loved Ones:** Loved ones who have passed often remain part of our support team, offering comfort and guidance. Their presence can bring a sense of closeness, reminding us that love transcends the boundaries of life and death. For example, I feel my mother's comforting energy at times, and my grandfather, who was knowledgeable in finances, seems to offer insight when I need practical guidance.

Additional Types of Spiritual Guides

Our spiritual team may also include:

❀ **Animal Guides:** Animals are frequently recognized in spiritual practices as potential messengers, each with symbolic meanings. Animal guides – like hawks symbolizing perspective or turtles signifying patience – can appear to remind us of qualities we may need to embody or messages relevant to our journey.

- **Ancestors:** Ancestors are considered a grounding influence in many spiritual teachings, providing a sense of connection to family and heritage. Their guidance is thought to support family matters, offering healing insights and wisdom from beyond.

Trusting the Process and Building Patience

Connecting with your spiritual team requires patience and trust. Like any relationship, it deepens over time. Don't be discouraged if you don't feel an immediate connection or sense of guidance. Trust the impressions you receive, no matter how small, as they are the building blocks of a deepening bond.

Over time, you may find communication with your guides growing stronger and more natural, bringing clarity to your intuition and enriching your journey.

My Experience with Angelic Guidance

One of my more vivid experiences with angelic reassurance came just before a weekend visit from my mother-in-law. Although I loved her dearly, I often felt a bit nervous about hosting her, as she could sometimes be challenging. In preparation, I said a quiet prayer to my angels, asking for a peaceful and joyful weekend without any unexpected incidents.

On the first evening of her visit, as I entered the living room – where she was sitting comfortably, watching TV – I was astonished to see thousands of tiny, twinkling lights shimmering across the ceiling, like stars filling the room. I knew instantly that my angels were with me, offering comfort and support.

The weekend unfolded beautifully, filled with happiness, laughter, and a sense of harmony among the family.

 **A Simple Way to Call on Your Angels**

You don't need fancy words or a special ritual to talk to your angels. They hear your thoughts, feel your heart, and respond with love. Whether you speak aloud, pray silently, or write your thoughts in a journal, what matters most is your sincerity.

Here's a simple prayer you might offer when seeking support:

Dear God and Angels,
Please surround me with your love and light.
Help me feel your presence, hear your guidance,
and trust my next steps.
Thank you for walking beside me.
Amen.

Speak from your heart and trust that your prayers have been heard. Be open to receiving their answers, even if they arrive in unexpected ways. Sometimes the most powerful guidance comes through quiet moments, gentle nudges, or the unfolding of time. All that's needed is a willingness to ask and to listen.

Recognizing Signs from Your Guides

Our spiritual support team often communicates through subtle, everyday signs – messages that gently remind us we are not alone. When we begin to notice patterns that feel too meaningful to ignore, it becomes clear that Spirit is reaching out.

These signs might show up as repeating numbers, unexpected feathers, meaningful song lyrics, or even animal encounters. They may also appear in dreams, art, or conversations that strike an emotional chord. The more we slow down and pay attention, the more easily we recognize the ways our guides are speaking to us.

Keeping a journal of these moments can help reveal recurring themes and strengthen your trust in their meaning. For instance:

❋ **Repeating Numbers:** Numbers like 1111, 222, or 444 are often seen as angel numbers – gentle reminders that you are supported and guided. But not all meaningful numbers are sequential. You may find yourself noticing a pattern like 479 showing up repeatedly – on receipts, license plates, or clocks. When a particular number keeps appearing, consider it a personal nudge from Spirit. Take a moment to reflect, or look up the numerological meaning for insight.

❋ **Feathers:** Finding a feather – especially in an unexpected place – is a common sign from the angels. It often appears as a message of comfort, encouragement, or divine presence. Many people report finding feathers during moments of grief, prayer, or transition, offering reassurance that their spiritual support team is near.

✸ **Songs or Lyrics:** Music is a powerful way Spirit gets our attention. A song might suddenly come to mind and play on the radio shortly after, or you may hear lyrics that speak directly to something you're going through. If a song stands out, try looking up the full lyrics – sometimes a line will leap off the page with a deeper message just for you.

✸ **Animal Messengers:** Animals are natural messengers from Spirit. When the same animal appears multiple times – either in person, artwork, or dreams – it often carries symbolic meaning. For instance, if you keep seeing butterflies in different forms, it may be a message about transformation and new beginnings. This might look like:

   ✻ A butterfly landing on your arm
   ✻ Seeing a butterfly on a postcard or billboard
   ✻ Having repeated dreams or memories of butterflies

Other animals carry their own wisdom. A hawk might invite you to see a situation from a higher perspective. A turtle may remind you to slow down and trust divine timing. Let your intuition guide you in understanding what the animal might represent in your life.

A Friend's Story: I have a friend who often receives messages at the movies. She told me, "It's amazing – I'll be watching a film, and it's like my soul is speaking to me through the storyline. There's always something in the characters or the dialogue that resonates so deeply with what I'm going through." For her, going to the movies isn't just about popcorn and entertainment – it's a spiritual experience, filled with signs, symbolism, and soul guidance.

Putting It All Together

When you notice a sign – a number, feather, song, animal, or something deeply personal – pause and reflect. Ask your guides for clarity and trust what you feel. A journal can help you keep track of signs and deepen your relationship with your spiritual team. Over time, you'll begin to see patterns and build a personal language with Spirit. The more you notice and acknowledge these signs, the more clearly they tend to show up. Spirit speaks often – all we need to do is listen.

Gratitude and Communication

Many spiritual teachings note that gratitude can strengthen the bond with our guides, keeping communication open and inviting further guidance. Simple gestures of appreciation, like journaling or lighting a candle, are believed to nurture this sacred connection. It is about your intention.

Exercises for Strengthening Your Connection

The following exercises are designed to help you deepen your relationship with your spiritual support team. Whether you're just beginning to explore this connection or seeking to strengthen it, these practices offer meaningful ways to invite their guidance into your daily life.

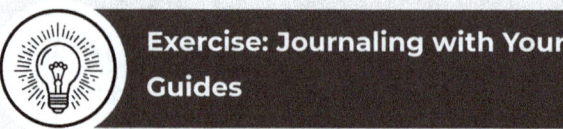

Exercise: Journaling with Your Guides

Purpose: To connect more deeply with your guides by asking questions and reflecting on their responses. This practice encourages trust and opens a channel for guidance.

Steps:

1. Find a quiet space where you won't be disturbed. Have your journal or a piece of paper ready.

2. Write a letter to your guides asking for guidance on a specific area of your life. Keep your tone open and conversational.

3. Spend a few minutes in meditation, allowing your mind to quiet and remaining receptive to any impressions or guidance.

4. After meditating, write down any thoughts, feelings, or symbols that came to you during the process. Reflect on how these impressions relate to your life.

Overcoming Doubt

When doubt arises, return to your center. Connecting with your guides is a process that unfolds over time. You don't need to have all the answers. Just be willing to trust the process and allow your soul to lead.

Use the SOUL method to gently reconnect:

Let Your SOUL Lead

Exercise: Asking for Validation

Purpose: To strengthen your trust in the messages you receive by seeking validation from your guides.

Steps:

- When you receive a message or impression from your guides, ask for a sign to validate the message (e.g., seeing a specific symbol or hearing a certain song).
- Record your request in your journal, noting the type of validation you asked for.
- Over the next few days, stay alert for signs or synchronicities that match your request.
- Reflect on how the validation appears and how it strengthens your connection with your guides.

S – Sit in stillness

O – Observe with openness

U – Understand that uncertainty is part of the journey

L – Let Spirit speak in its own way and timing

Your willingness to sit, listen, trust, and allow creates the space for guidance to come through. Even if signs or messages are subtle at first, they will grow clearer with patience, presence, and faith.

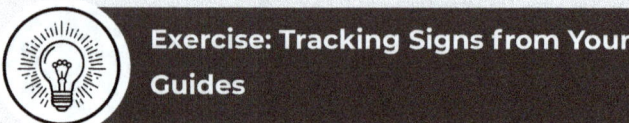

Exercise: Tracking Signs from Your Guides

Purpose: To heighten your awareness of subtle signs and patterns from your guides, building trust in their communication.

Steps:

1. Begin keeping a journal specifically for signs and synchronicities.

2. Each day, note any repeating numbers, symbols, or other meaningful occurrences you observe.

3. Reflect on how these patterns connect to questions or challenges in your life.

4. Use your journal entries to recognize recurring themes and deepen your understanding of your guides' communication style.

 **Exercise: Daily Check-In Meditation**

Purpose: To create a regular practice of connecting with your guides and receiving intuitive guidance.

Close your eyes and take three deep breaths, allowing yourself to release any tension and find your center. Envision a warm, golden light surrounding you, filling your space with peace and tranquility. When you feel ready, ask your guides a simple question, such as, "What do I need to focus on today?" or "What guidance do you have for me?" Remain still and listen for any impressions, words, or images that come to mind. Afterward, take a few moments to write down your experience in your journal and reflect on how it might relate to your day ahead.

Sample Meditation for Connecting with Your Guides

If you're ready to take your connection with your guides a step further, this guided meditation offers a peaceful and intentional way to invite their presence and wisdom into your life.

Find a comfortable spot, close your eyes, and relax. Envision a golden light filling your entire being, bringing a sense of peace and calm. As you breathe in this light, let it wash over you, releasing any tension or stress.

Now, imagine a door in front of you. Step through and find yourself in a beautiful, sunlit garden. The fragrance of flowers fills the air, and you hear the soft hum of nature around you. At the center of the garden, there's a comfortable bench. Sit down and relax, feeling deeply at peace.

Soon, you sense the presence of one of your guides. Whether you see them as light or a distinct form, trust what you experience. Ask simple questions, such as, "How are you helping me? What are the signs you send?" Allow yourself to receive their responses, whether as words, impressions, or feelings.

When you're ready, thank your guide for their wisdom. Return through the door, wiggling your fingers and toes, and open your eyes, feeling refreshed. Take a few moments to journal about your experience.

Free guided meditation
"Meet Your Spirit Guides"
Download at:
LoriSheridanMedium.com/soulgift

Personal Stories of Connection

One of my most memorable validations of a guide's presence came from a spirit artist who drew a portrait of one of my guides. Though I had glimpsed her in meditation before, the likeness was astonishing – her curly hair, warm eyes, and confident energy were captured perfectly. This visual connection reminded me of her constant presence and offered deep reassurance of her support.

Another guide, who has introduced himself to me in meditation as Red Feather, has found unique ways to say hello over the years. Once, a mediumship student came to class and asked me point-blank, "Do you have a guide named Red Feather?" I was surprised and replied, "Yes, I do. Why?" She told me he had appeared to her in meditation, letting her know he worked with me and was helping her as well. I smiled, as I had never shared his name with anyone. On another occasion, in a mediumship development class, a different student handed me a red hawk feather. "I'm not sure why," he said, "but when I saw this, I knew I needed to give it to you." I smiled, sensing once again that this was Red Feather's playful way of reaching out to me.

Soul Takeaways and Inspired Action

You are never alone. From the moment you arrived in this world, a loving spiritual support team has walked beside you, offering guidance, protection, and encouragement through life's twists and turns.

Your connection with this team is a relationship that grows over time. Like any friendship, it deepens with presence, trust, and intention. The more you invite their support and acknowledge their signs, the more clearly their messages begin to unfold.

There is no perfect way to communicate. Speak from your heart. Ask for a sign. Sit in stillness. Keep a journal of your experiences. Whether you sense them through numbers, music, animals, or quiet knowing, trust that these nudges are real and meant for you.

When doubt arises, come back to your **SOUL**:

Sit with openness.

Observe the signs.

Understand that guidance may arrive gently and in divine timing.

Let Spirit Speak in its own way.

Your guides are part of your soul's journey. Their love is unwavering, their messages are rooted in gentle support, and their presence is a quiet reassurance that you are seen, guided, and deeply loved. Even when life feels uncertain, they are there holding your hand from the other side, walking beside you with grace and devotion.

Timeless Wisdom

"We are never alone. Invisible hands are guiding us, silent hearts are loving us, and unseen friends are walking beside us."
– White Eagle

Your spiritual support team is closer than you think.
In moments of stillness, their presence becomes clear.
Trust the warmth, the signs, the quiet knowing.
Love is always reaching out from the other side.

"The presence of those
we love never truly leaves
us. They walk beside us,
unseen, unheard, but
always near."
– Anonymous

Chapter 9
Mediumship: Connecting with Spirit

*H*ave you ever felt an unexpected warmth wash over you, as if an invisible embrace were surrounding you, or sensed a comforting presence during a time of need? These subtle, heartfelt moments are often the Spirit world's way of reminding us that love is eternal and that our loved ones are never far. Mediumship is a way to open that door – to reach out across the divide and feel the connection that continues beyond this life.

Mediumship isn't about special gifts given to a chosen few. It's a natural ability that lives within all of us – part of our soul's eternal connection to Source and to one another.

Like learning to play an instrument, some may find that mediumship comes naturally, while others develop it more gradually with practice and patience. Whether you're playing simple melodies or a full symphony, each moment of connection is sacred.

Mediumship is the bridge between the physical and the spiritual, offering healing, comfort, and the reassurance that we are never truly alone. Through mediumship, we discover that love never dies and that those who have passed are still here, walking beside us, offering guidance, and celebrating our joys.

In this chapter, we'll explore what it means to connect with Spirit. You'll learn to recognize the signs that you might have a natural affinity for mediumship, discover ways to strengthen your connection with loved ones in spirit, and understand how to receive the messages that they lovingly offer. Whether you're seeking comfort, hope, or simply the feeling that those you cherish are still near, this chapter will guide you in opening your heart to the Spirit world.

Each soul's path to Spirit is unique – and wherever you are on your journey, your willingness to explore is enough. Trust that your connection, no matter how it unfolds, is exactly as it should be.

Discovering and Nurturing Your Connection

If you're drawn to the Spirit world, you may already be sensing the natural connection that exists within you. Mediumship is about building a bridge between this world and the world of spirit, inviting loving communication from those who have passed.

Sometimes, this awareness emerges gently over time; other times, it may awaken more vividly during seasons of transformation or major life events. However it unfolds, trust that your connection is real – and that with patience, practice, and an open heart, it can grow stronger.

My Personal Journey

My own journey with mediumship began in childhood. In some of my earliest memories, I can remember watching colored lights dance across my bedroom ceiling, feeling the loving presence of the Spirit world as I drifted off to sleep. At other times, while walking in the woods near my childhood home, I would sense that I wasn't alone. Though I couldn't see anyone, I felt a comforting presence beside me, as if someone was walking quietly with me. Over the years, this sense of companionship grew, and I would sometimes wake in the night, seeing or feeling the presence of departed loved ones watching over me. Still, it wasn't until after college that I truly allowed myself to explore this connection through formal classes in psychic and mediumship development. Each step has been one of discovery, showing me that the Spirit world is closer than I once believed and that in this journey, we are held by unseen hands, guiding and supporting us every step of the way.

Signs You May Be Naturally In Tune with Spirit

Mediumship is a natural ability that many people are drawn to, often without even realizing it. Some individuals may simply be more sensitive or attuned to the presence of Spirit, especially during certain seasons of life. Here are a few signs that might suggest a natural awareness or openness to this kind of connection:

- ✸ Vivid dreams or premonitions that later come true.
- ✸ Sensing the presence of a loved one who has passed –

feeling their warmth, hearing their voice, or smelling a familiar scent.

- Hearing your name called when no one is there, or hearing a voice that feels familiar and comforting.
- Childhood experiences with imaginary friends or feeling a strong sense of connection to the unseen.
- Seeing lights, shadows, or faces in your peripheral vision or your mind's eye that others might not notice.
- Feeling energy shifts in certain places, especially in rooms where significant events have occurred.
- A natural attraction to spiritual teachings, the paranormal, or intuitive tools like tarot, crystals, or meditation.
- Unusual electronic malfunctions that seem tied to your presence, such as flickering lights or disrupted phone signals.
- A family history of spirit communication, where other relatives have also had psychic or mediumship abilities.

If some of these resonate, you may be naturally more in tune with the subtle energy of the Spirit world. But remember, mediumship isn't reserved for a gifted few – it's something we can all explore. With patience, practice, and a willingness to listen, this connection can grow stronger over time. Often, it unfolds gently and beautifully, in perfect divine timing.

Understanding Mediumship

Mediumship is the ability to connect with the Spirit world, sharing evidence of life beyond our physical existence. Through mediumship, a spirit medium may receive details like names, memories, personalities, or shared experiences that validate a departed loved one's presence. The ultimate purpose is to offer comfort, hope, and healing – a reminder that love never dies.

Mediums use their intuitive senses, such as clairvoyance (seeing), clairsentience (feeling), and clairaudience (hearing), to build a bridge with the Spirit world.

These same senses can be used psychically to tune into people's energy here and now, but in mediumship, they are lovingly directed toward blending with the soul of a loved one who has crossed over, allowing their messages to come through.

During a reading, the medium's energy gently rises or "quickens," while the spirit communicator's energy softens, creating a shared vibration where communication becomes possible.

It's a bit like tuning into a special radio station. The Spirit world vibrates at a higher frequency, a beautiful wavelength of love. As we lift our energy upward and the spirit lowers theirs just a little, we meet – and the heart-to-heart connection unfolds naturally through love, trust, and intention.

Connecting with Loved Ones for Comfort and Healing

Whether you identify as a medium or simply want to feel closer to a loved one, there are ways to invite their presence into your life. Here are a few methods to try, from dream visitations to recognizing meaningful signs. In addition to these approaches, the following exercises can help you build and deepen your connection with Spirit, creating opportunities for healing, guidance, and love.

❋ **Dream Visitations:** Loved ones often reach out through dreams. These "visitation dreams" feel distinctly different – more vivid and real. You might sit across from your loved one, talk, or feel their familiar warmth. If you've experienced a dream like this, know that it was a real visit. You can encourage more of these experiences by setting an intention before bed and asking for a visit. Keep a journal nearby to capture any feelings, words, or images upon waking.

❋ **Signs and Synchronicities:** Our loved ones use signs to communicate with us, such as feathers, coins, birds, or familiar songs. These signs often appear at just the right moment, bringing a sense of reassurance or comfort. If you notice these signs, trust that they are meant for you. Accept them as reminders that your loved one is still near, offering support and guidance from beyond.

Personal Story: A Scent from Heaven

During a difficult period in my life, I often found myself feeling uncertain and overwhelmed. One day, while sitting in my car, I suddenly noticed the familiar scent of my grandfather's cologne. It was as though he was sitting beside me, and the scent enveloped me like a warm embrace, offering comfort and reassurance just as he had in life. Over the next few weeks, this scent would reappear each time I needed it most, reminding me that my grandfather's spirit was near, helping me find peace and the strength to carry on. That subtle scent became a reminder of his love and unwavering support, even from the other side.

Spirit's Gentle Language

- ✺ A sudden scent that fills the room.
- ✺ A song that plays at just the right moment.
- ✺ A warm embrace felt in a dream.
- ✺ A soft nudge to keep going.

The Spirit world speaks in whispers. Trust what you feel, and know that love is always reaching out to meet you.

Developing Your Connection: Trust and Patience

Connecting with loved ones in spirit is like building a relationship. It takes trust, patience, and openness to the ways they communicate. Sometimes, the signs are immediate, but other times they come in unexpected moments. Trust that even if you don't receive signs right away, your loved ones are listening and supporting you from beyond.

Exercises for Strengthening Your Connection

Deepening your bond with the Spirit world requires practice, trust, and a willingness to explore the ways your loved ones communicate. These exercises are designed to help you open your heart, recognize signs, and cultivate meaningful connections with those in spirit. Whether you're just beginning or seeking to refine your abilities, each practice offers an opportunity to invite love, healing, and guidance into your life.

Exercise: Asking for a Sign

Purpose: To build your connection by inviting a clear sign from a loved one in spirit. This practice fosters trust and recognition of how they communicate.

Steps:

1. Find a quiet moment and ask your loved one for a specific sign. For example, you might say, "Please send me a sign that I'll recognize as coming from you."

2. Be open to receiving signs over the next few days, such as hearing a meaningful song, seeing a specific animal, or feeling a warm sensation.

3. Record these experiences in your journal, noting the timing, type of sign, and any emotions you felt.

4. Reflect on how these signs align with your intention and deepen your connection to your loved one.

Exercise: Writing a Letter

Purpose: To foster communication with a loved one in spirit by expressing your thoughts and opening yourself to receive their guidance.

Steps:

1. Set aside a quiet, peaceful space with your journal or a piece of paper.

2. Write a heartfelt letter to your loved one, sharing your feelings, memories, or questions.

3. After writing, sit quietly and meditate, focusing on your loved one's presence.

4. Allow any impressions, words, or images to come to mind, and write them down as a response.

5. Reflect on this exchange, noting any comfort or clarity it brought you.

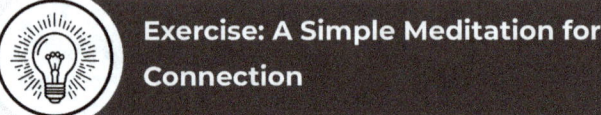

Exercise: A Simple Meditation for Connection

Purpose: To invite a loving connection with a departed loved one through visualization.

Find a quiet, comfortable space and gently close your eyes, allowing your breath to guide you into a state of relaxation. Picture yourself stepping onto a stunning, serene beach, where the soft, golden sand warms your feet, and the rhythmic sound of waves gently lapping at the shore soothes your spirit. The salty breeze carries with it a sense of peace, brushing against your skin as the sunlight dances on the water's surface. As you walk slowly along the shore, feel the steady grounding of the earth beneath you. Ahead, you notice a figure approaching – a loved one who has passed. Their presence grows clearer with each step, radiating warmth and love. When you meet, feel their familiar embrace, a connection as real and comforting as it was in life. Share with them whatever is on your heart, whether through words, thoughts, or simply your presence together. When the time feels right, bid them farewell for now, knowing their love continues to walk with you. As you turn back along the shore, feel their light and warmth surrounding you, offering peace and reassurance. When you're ready, gently open your eyes and take a moment to journal your experience, capturing any words, images, or emotions that came through.

Trusting the Process

Mediumship is a journey of trust. With time and practice, your connection with the Spirit world can deepen, allowing messages to come through with more clarity and confidence. Even if you don't feel a direct presence right away, your loved ones are only a thought away – ready to offer their love and support whenever you need it. Each time you open your heart to Spirit, you strengthen a relationship that continues beyond the physical, carried by love.

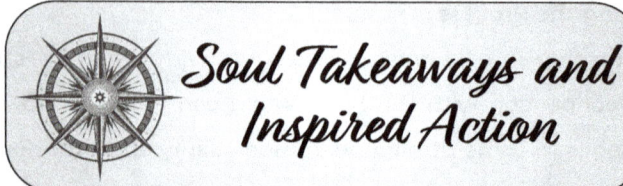

Soul Takeaways and Inspired Action

Mediumship is a sacred invitation to recognize that the soul lives on and that our connection with those we love transcends the physical. Each time we pause, open our hearts, and listen, we strengthen our bond with the Spirit world.

You don't have to call yourself a medium to receive signs, feel a presence, or be moved by the unseen. Simply holding space for the possibility of connection can create room for love, healing, and peace to flow in.

Trust what you feel. Whether it's a whisper in your heart, a vivid dream, or the scent of a loved one's cologne, these experiences are meaningful. Spirit communicates in many ways – through feelings, thoughts, images, and energy. As you grow in awareness, you'll begin to recognize the subtle language of the soul.

This journey isn't about perfection. It's about building trust – within yourself and with those in spirit. Like any relationship, it deepens with time, attention, and love. Your desire to connect is enough to begin.

Start simply. Journal your experiences, ask for signs, speak to your loved ones, and notice what stirs within you. Even small moments of connection can offer profound comfort and validation.

Above all, know this: Love never dies. It transforms, expands, and continues to walk beside us, lighting the way. As you explore the Spirit world, may you feel held, supported, and guided by the invisible threads of love that bind us all.

Timeless Wisdom

"There is no death.
The Spirit can never die.
It always was and
always will be."
– Silver Birch

Mediumship reminds us that love and life are eternal. Each message from Spirit is a gentle whisper of this truth, offering comfort, hope, and the reassurance that those we love walk beside us still. Trust the signs, the presence, and the quiet knowing that connection never ends.

"What you think, you create.
What you feel, you attract. What
you imagine, you become."
– Anonymous

Chapter 10
Manifesting Your Desires with Intuition

*I*magine waking up every morning knowing that the life you dream of is not only possible, but that you hold the power to create it. Every thought, feeling, and intention you carry can help shape your reality. Manifestation is not just a concept; it's an invitation to co-create with the universe, to bring your deepest desires to life by aligning with the powerful energy of your own intuition.

Manifestation and intuition go hand in hand. While intuition guides us toward the choices that align with our highest path, manifestation is about using that inner compass to intentionally shape the world around us. By trusting both our inner guidance and the limitless potential of the universe, we can actively participate in the creation of a life filled with joy, abundance, and purpose.

The beauty of manifestation lies in its simplicity and accessibility – it is available to everyone, at every moment. You don't need anything special, just an open heart and the willingness to trust yourself. When we align our intentions, thoughts, and emotions with our soul's desires, we begin to see the world transform in magical and surprising ways.

In this chapter, we'll explore how to harness the power of manifestation using our intuition as a guide. We'll dive into practical techniques, exercises, and personal stories that show how small changes in our thinking and feeling can lead to profound shifts in our reality. Let's journey together and discover how, with the universe as your partner, you can create a life that aligns beautifully with your dreams.

The Art of Manifestation

Manifestation is about consciously focusing your energy and intention to draw in the experiences you truly desire. It's more than simply thinking positively or wishing for the best. It's a co-creative process with the universe that involves setting clear intentions, trusting in your inner power, and taking inspired action.

Inspired action is the inner nudge or quiet knowing that guides you toward the next right step – something that feels aligned with your heart and your vision. It bridges the gap between dreaming and doing. When you combine intention with small, meaningful steps, you build momentum that tells both your soul and the universe you're ready.

It's also important that your desires feel believable and aligned with where you are now. This doesn't mean limiting your dreams; it means giving them strong roots. When your goals feel emotionally true and energetically possible, your mind and body work together to support their unfolding. You can absolutely grow into something big and beautiful, but every dream begins with a step you can say yes to today.

By honoring your role as a co-creator, and working in partnership with the universe – a supportive force that responds to your energy and intention – you empower yourself to shape your reality with clarity, confidence, and grace.

Clarity Is Key

To manifest, the first step is becoming crystal clear about what you truly want and why. The universe responds most strongly to clear intentions. When you know what you desire, you create a powerful, magnetic focus that draws the right opportunities, people, and experiences into your life. Setting clear intentions acts as a signal to the universe, letting it know that you're ready and committed.

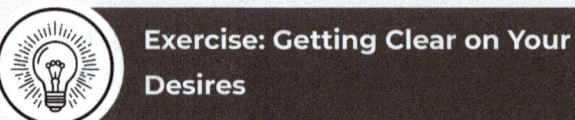

Exercise: Getting Clear on Your Desires

Purpose: To clarify your desires, making it easier for the universe to respond to your intentions.

Steps:

1. Find a quiet space where you can reflect without distractions.

2. Ask yourself: *What do I genuinely desire and why?* Write your goals or dreams as clearly as possible, focusing on key areas like relationships, career, health, and personal growth.

3. Write your desires in the present tense, as if they are already manifesting, such as: "I am thriving in a career that excites and fulfills me."

4. Revisit your written desires often, refining them as your vision evolves. Reflect on how this practice brings clarity to your intentions.

Intuition as a Manifestation Compass

Our intuition is a powerful ally in the manifestation process, guiding us toward the right opportunities, people, and steps that bring our desires closer. By following intuitive nudges – a sudden urge to connect with someone, a dream that brings clarity, or a meaningful synchronicity – we align ourselves with the flow of the universe.

Think of your intuition as your internal compass, pointing you toward your desires in subtle yet powerful ways. As you work to manifest your goals, staying attuned to the small signs and whispers of your intuition amplifies your ability to manifest with ease and trust. These intuitive messages often show up when we least expect them, and being open to them can bring remarkable changes.

Exercise: Tuning into Intuitive Messages

Purpose: To strengthen your manifestation process by using intuition as a guide.

Steps:

1. Before bed or during meditation, focus on a specific desire.

2. Ask the universe or your guides for a sign or insight to lead you closer to your goal.

3. Pay attention to symbols, dreams, or feelings that arise over the next few days.

4. Write your impressions in a journal. Reflect on how these messages align with your desires and guide your next steps.

The Power of Emotion in Manifestation

Emotion is one of the most powerful forces in the manifestation process. When we hold our desires with positive emotions – such as excitement, gratitude, and joy – we magnify our intentions and create an energetic alignment that draws those desires closer. If thoughts are the seeds of manifestation, emotions are the sunlight and water that help those seeds grow. The emotional energy behind our intentions creates a powerful magnetism that the universe responds to.

Visualization Practice

Each day, take a few moments to visualize your desires as if they are already happening. Imagine how it would feel to be living your ideal reality. Picture the sights, sounds, and feelings, immersing yourself in that experience. This visualization practice helps to shift your energy and align your current state with your goals, making it easier for the universe to bring your desires to you. Visualize not only the outcome but also the process that takes you there, allowing yourself to feel the joy of each step.

The Power of Vision Boards

Each January, I set aside a little time to create a vision board for the year ahead – a visual representation of the dreams I hold for myself, my family, and my work. It's a creative and intuitive process that helps bring clarity and intention to my goals.

I'm not one for cutting and pasting from magazines, so I usually create my vision board digitally using a simple design program like Microsoft Word, Canva, or PicMonkey. I add photos, phrases, and meaningful words that reflect what I want to experience or call into my life. Then, I print it out and hang it on my wall next to my desk where I'll see it every day.

There's something powerful about seeing your dreams displayed in front of you. It keeps you focused, motivated, and in alignment with the energy of what you're calling in. Last year, for example, I included an image that represented becoming a contributing author – and not long after, I had the opportunity to share a story in the published book *Signs & Synchronicities: True Stories That Inspire and Empower*. I also visualized travel for work, and soon I found myself serving in new states and communities.

It's amazing what can unfold when you align your energy, set an intention, and take small, inspired steps forward. A vision board may seem simple, but it's a powerful tool that speaks directly to your soul – and to the universe.

Personal Story: Visualizing Success

When I first began my career as a medium, I had no idea where it would lead or how I would be of service. During meditation, I often practiced visualization and asked myself: *How am I meant to serve, and what will my work look like in the future?* I would imagine having my own office, seeing clients, and teaching classes. I saw myself serving Spiritualist churches, offering public demonstrations, and being invited to teach at metaphysical centers. I held these visions with excitement, seeing myself confident and at ease, even though I was unsure of how to make them a reality. With each visualization, I felt more reassured. Over time, these visions began to manifest in real ways. Now, when I look back, I see that visualizing my goals, in partnership with my intuition, played a significant role in creating these meaningful experiences. It was the joy, confidence, and belief in the vision that helped to transform those dreams into reality.

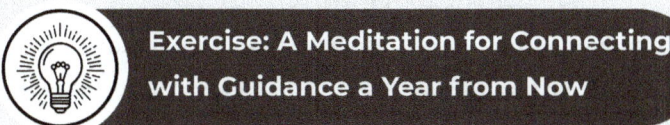

Exercise: A Meditation for Connecting with Guidance a Year from Now

Purpose: To explore your future potential and gain intuitive insight into the year ahead.

Settle into a quiet space and focus on your breath. Envision a golden light of unconditional love surrounding you. As you relax, imagine a door appearing before you. Step through it and find yourself in a beautiful library filled with books on every topic imaginable. In this library, a wise guide awaits you. They welcome you and hand you a special book, one that holds insights into the year ahead. Ask your guide to open this book and show you what your life looks like one year from now. See yourself living in alignment with your dreams, fulfilling your highest potential. Take note of any messages or images that arise, and express gratitude for this glimpse into the future. Slowly return to the present, bringing with you the wisdom of this experience.

Letting Go of Limiting Beliefs

One of the greatest obstacles to manifesting our desires is the presence of limiting beliefs – those internalized thoughts and patterns that quietly whisper, "I'm not good enough," "I don't deserve this," or "That's not possible for someone like me." These beliefs can block the flow of manifestation by sending mixed signals to the universe, creating resistance even when our intentions are clear.

It's important to remember that doubt is a natural part of the journey. We all carry fears and inner stories, many of which aren't truly ours. Some were shaped in childhood or inherited from those around us, born in moments when we didn't feel seen, safe, or supported. Over time, these outdated beliefs can become embedded in our thinking, influencing how we see ourselves and what we believe is possible.

Gently uncovering and transforming these patterns can be a powerful act of self-love. Journaling, meditation, quiet reflection, and prayer can all offer insight into the stories we carry. Taking time to notice what no longer feels true opens the door to a more authentic way of living. Working with a counselor, spiritual mentor, or coach can also be a meaningful way to explore these patterns with compassion and perspective. Whether we do this inner work independently or with support, it becomes a sacred opportunity to reconnect with our highest self and align with what truly matters.

Think of your mind as a garden. The beliefs you hold are the seeds. Some have been planted without your awareness, and some have grown into patterns that no longer serve you. But the best part is this: you can continue to learn, plant new seeds, branch out in fresh directions, and make changes as needed. You are the keeper of your garden. With care, attention, and a willingness to grow, you can cultivate a mindset that reflects your soul's truth and the life you wish to live.

We can live with mindfulness and choose to go within, asking for guidance to help us recognize outdated patterns and make loving, empowered choices. Through prayer, meditation, and spiritual reflection, we can receive support from the universe, from our loved ones in spirit, and from the divine presence that walks beside us every day.

Exercise: Releasing Limiting Beliefs

Purpose: To identify and release limiting beliefs, creating space for aligned manifestation.

Steps:

1. Write down any recurring thoughts that feel limiting or self-critical.

2. Ask yourself: *Where did this belief come from? Is it still true for me?*

3. Gently challenge the belief. What would a more loving or supportive truth sound like?

4. Create affirmations that uplift and align with your desired future (e.g., *I am worthy of success, Abundance flows to me with ease, I trust myself to make aligned decisions*).

5. Repeat these affirmations regularly, even if they feel unfamiliar at first. Over time, they will begin to shift your energy and reshape your reality.

6. Use journaling or meditation to explore any emotions that arise. Invite insights, patterns, or memories into your awareness with curiosity and compassion. You might ask yourself: *What am I ready to release? How can I respond to this situation with greater love?*

Personal Story: Moving Past My Own Limiting Beliefs

Years ago, I often found myself asking: *Am I really good enough to do this work?* Fear and doubt would creep in, especially as I began serving publicly. What if I wasn't enough?

Through positive affirmations, prayer, and the encouragement of friends, teachers, clients, and Spirit, I began to shift my perspective. I reminded myself that I didn't have to be perfect, I just had to be present and trust. Spirit has a way of meeting us where we are, sending the right people and opportunities at the right time. As I began to trust myself and the divine timing of the universe, doors opened in ways I never could have predicted. These experiences have taught me the incredible power of belief in shaping our path and the importance of trusting ourselves and the unfolding journey.

Personal Story: Shifting My Beliefs About Abundance

When my husband and I bought our home, we scraped together just enough for the down payment. Money was tight, and I vividly remember lying awake at night worrying, *Would we have enough money to pay the mortgage? Could we support our growing family? Would we be okay?*

That time in our lives forced me to examine my beliefs about money and self-worth. I had internalized scarcity thinking and inherited fears that whispered, *There's never enough.* Slowly, I began to shift those thoughts and replace them with new intentions rooted in trust.

A dear friend shared an affirmation with me that I still say to this day: "*I am in the flow of infinite abundance. I am always provided for. The right people and opportunities find me at just the right time. I have all I need and more. I am infinitely supported.*"

At first, it felt like just words. But I said them anyway. I made small savings goals, became more mindful of my thoughts and habits, and gently redirected the negative patterns when they arose. Over time, not only did my mindset shift – so did my cash flow. The more I trusted, the more support I received, and the easier it became to move forward with a sense of ease and faith.

Another teacher once shared something I've never forgotten: There is no need for competition. There is more than enough abundance for everyone to have what they need. Now, when I see someone enjoying something I admire, I say softly to the universe, "*God bless. Yes, I'd love that too.*"

I also remind myself that a flower doesn't worry about how fast or beautifully the others around it are blooming – it simply opens when it's ready, in its own time, just as it's meant to. And just like in any garden, it's the diversity of blooms, each one unique, that creates the richness and beauty of the whole. That simple truth helps me return to trust again and again.

By acknowledging and releasing the beliefs that no longer serve us, we create space for the life we truly want to live. Whether through gentle reflection, spiritual practice, or supported guidance, we return again and again to the knowing that we are whole, we are worthy, and we are co-creators of our lives. Growth is not a destination but a living, unfolding path, and we are always being invited to tend our inner garden with love.

Just as I began to shift my own beliefs around money and trust the flow of abundance, I was inspired by a close friend whose manifesting journey reminded me how powerful intention can truly be.

A Friend's Story: Manifesting in the Flow

I have a dear friend who I jokingly call a "manifesting guru" because she has what I describe as the Midas touch – if she thinks it and believes it, it happens. She once set the intention to start manifesting more money for fun things. Almost immediately, she began noticing a steady stream of unexpected "fun money" arriving in the form of $20 bills. It was as if the universe had heard her loud and clear.

Encouraged by her results, she decided to dream a little bigger. Her daughter was engaged, and she thought, "I'd love to gift her the wedding dress of her dreams." She knew she'd need a more significant amount of money – and she wanted it to be set aside, not spent easily – so she specifically asked the universe to send her $100 bills to help her save. Over the next few weeks, she began receiving exactly that: $100 bills, one after another, until she had $1,700 – the exact amount she needed to buy the dress. Her daughter was overjoyed, and it was a memory they'll both treasure forever.

Since then, she's kept up the practice of saving her $100 bills. And interestingly, she's noticed that whenever the flow seems to slow down, it often shifts again when she gives from the heart. Whether treating her kids to a little something special or using the money to bless someone else, she finds that the moment she releases the energy, it returns – often multiplied.

Her story is a beautiful reminder that setting clear intentions, staying in the flow, and giving with love can create powerful shifts – sometimes in ways more magical than we imagined.

Trusting the Timing of the Universe

Manifestation doesn't always follow our ideal timeline. We may set clear intentions, take meaningful action, and still find ourselves waiting. But that doesn't mean nothing is happening. Sometimes, the very thing we're longing for is already on its way – we just haven't caught up to it yet.

In many ways, time is a social construct, a framework we use to measure progress and productivity. But the soul operates beyond clocks and calendars. In the greater unfolding of life, everything is happening exactly as it should. Delays are often detours that lead us to something better prepared, more aligned, and deeply meant for us. What's unfolding behind the scenes may be the very foundation needed to support the life we are growing into.

Think of the crocus, buried beneath the frozen ground. For months, there's no sign of life on the surface, yet deep beneath the soil, it's slowly preparing to bloom. And then, one day in spring, it rises – bright and beautiful, just as it was meant to. We don't always see our growth as it's happening, but that doesn't mean it's not unfolding. Like the crocus, our transformation begins in the quiet, unseen places.

We are not the same person we were five years ago, ten years ago, or even one day ago. Change is a constant. Time is continual. And in that flow, we are always becoming.

When we let go of the need to control every detail, we create space for the universe to work in ways that often surprise and bless us. Trusting divine timing is one of the most sacred invitations of this journey.

Personal Story: When the Universe Opens the Door

Several years ago, our family came to a difficult realization: the school setting our son was in no longer felt supportive or sustainable. Despite our ongoing efforts and many conversations, it became clear that in order for him to truly thrive, we would need to seek out a new environment – one with more resources, understanding, and room to grow.

It was not a decision we took lightly. The idea of leaving our home, our friends, and the life we had built was daunting. But we prayed for guidance. Deep in my heart, I heard a voice say clearly: *He will never get what he needs here. It's time to go.*

Although I know this isn't an option every family can consider, for us, it became a deeply personal calling – one that required courage, faith, and a willingness to start fresh. My husband and I both knew, deep down, that this was the path forward.

What happened next felt undeniably guided. Within a week of putting our house on the market, we received an offer well above our asking price at our very first open house. That opened the door for us to leap. Things moved quickly. We found our next home with ease, and before we knew it, we were moving in just in time for the start of the school year.

And it was there, in that new beginning, that we found what we had been hoping for. Our son's new school was filled with educators and staff who truly saw him – who met him where he was and began opening doors that had previously felt sealed shut. They helped bridge the gap between potential and possibility. We watched him begin to grow in ways we hadn't dared to imagine.

The journey was long – and in truth, it's still unfolding. It didn't happen overnight. But it reminded me in the most powerful way that divine timing is real. And when we listen to the voice within and take brave, aligned steps forward, the universe has a way of rising up to meet us with extraordinary grace.

Rejection as Redirection

Sometimes, a "no" is simply a form of protection or redirection. When things don't go as planned, it's natural to feel disappointed. But what if that no is actually making space for something better?

Rejection isn't a failure – it's feedback. It's an opportunity for self-reflection, a moment to pause and gently consider whether what we were asking for truly supports where we're headed. These moments can offer deep insight and open the door to new possibilities we might not have considered.

When we can approach these experiences from a space of nonjudgment, we begin to trust that everything is unfolding for our highest good. We may not always understand the timing or the outcome, but we can trust that the universe has our back and is working with us, not against us.

Sometimes, we have to be willing to let go of what we thought we wanted in order to make room for the unseen blessings on the way. And often, what arrives is even more beautiful than what we imagined.

Taking Inspired Action

Manifestation is about more than just thinking and feeling; it also involves taking inspired action. Inspired action means following through on those inner nudges that feel aligned with your goals, even if they seem small or uncertain. The universe often opens doors in unexpected ways, guiding us toward our dreams. By acting on these intuitive impulses, we take steps that bring our visions into reality.

Exercise: Small Steps, Big Results

Purpose: To take concrete actions that align with your manifestations.

Steps:

1. Identify one small step you can take today to move closer to your desires.

2. Write down one or two actions and commit to completing them.

3. Reflect on how these actions bring you closer to your goal and build momentum toward your dreams.

Gratitude: The Secret Ingredient

Gratitude is one of the most powerful forces in manifestation. When we focus on what we're grateful for, we align with the energy of abundance. This shift invites more of what we desire into our lives. Acknowledging the blessings we receive, even the small ones, creates a positive cycle of attraction and reception. Gratitude helps us stay in a state of openness and receptivity, making it easier for the universe to bring us what we need.

Quick Manifesting Story: The Power of Asking

Around the holidays, I like to call on my "parking angels" for a little assistance with the seasonal hustle and bustle. I'll ask for help finding a good spot close to the entrance – and more often than not, one opens up just when I need it. It's become a fun tradition, and it reminds me that a little positive intention goes a long way.

I'll do the same when going out to dinner with my family, quietly asking that we quickly get a cozy booth, even in a packed restaurant. And yes, my husband teases me because I even ask for help when trying to make left-hand turns on busy streets. I'll whisper, "Okay angels, a little break in traffic, please," and sure enough, a pause appears and I can safely make my way through the intersection.

These small, everyday requests are light-hearted, but they reflect a powerful truth: when we ask for help – whether it's for a parking space or peace in our lives – we open the door to support. A little faith, a little hope, and a sense of gratitude can turn even the simplest moments into reminders that we're not doing life alone.

From the tiniest daily needs to heartfelt prayers for our family, friends, and the communities in which we live and work, the universe is always listening. And when we ask with love and a grateful heart, help has a beautiful way of showing up.

Exercise: Gratitude Journal

Purpose: To align with the energy of abundance and attract more positive experiences.

Steps:

1. Keep a journal dedicated to gratitude.
2. Write down three things you're thankful for each day and explain why.
3. Reflect on how focusing on gratitude enhances your overall sense of abundance and well-being.

Trusting Yourself and the Universe

Manifestation is not only about achieving specific outcomes; it's about becoming the kind of person who aligns with those outcomes. As you set intentions and align with them, you'll find yourself evolving in ways that bring you closer to the life you want to create. Trust yourself, trust the process, and remember that the universe is always working with you. With each step toward your dreams, you are co-creating a life that reflects your highest potential. Trust in the magic of the universe and in your own ability to bring your dreams to life, knowing that every effort, no matter how small, is moving you closer to your goals.

Soul Takeaways and Inspired Action

Manifestation is a sacred act of remembering who you are and what you are capable of creating. It's not about forcing outcomes or chasing perfection, but about gently aligning with the quiet wisdom of your soul and allowing the universe to meet you there. Each intention you set, each small step you take, sends a signal that you're ready to receive – not just what you think you want, but what is truly meant for you.

This journey begins with clarity – getting honest about your desires and allowing yourself to dream from the heart. As you open to the possibilities that live within you, your intuition will begin to light the way, guiding you through gentle nudges, synchronicities, and inner knowing. Trust that you don't need to have it all figured out. You just need to say yes to the next step.

It's also natural for doubts to arise. Old beliefs may surface, but these, too, are part of the process. With compassion and awareness, you can begin to release the stories that no longer serve you and plant new ones that reflect your worth, your truth, and your vision for what's possible. Every moment of reflection, every affirmation spoken in hope, is a step toward something greater.

Know that timing is its own kind of grace. You may not always understand why something hasn't arrived yet, but trust that growth is happening – even when you can't see it. Like the crocus blooming beneath the soil, much of our transformation unfolds in the unseen. When we trust the process, stay present, and remain open, the path forward begins to reveal itself in divine and beautiful ways.

Whether you're manifesting a new beginning or simply inviting more peace into your day, remember that you are never alone. The universe is always listening, always responding, and always guiding you. The more you practice gratitude, speak your truth, and act on what feels right in your heart, the more you allow miracles – small and large – to find their way to you.

You are already manifesting with every breath, every thought, and every choice. Trust your journey, listen within, and know that your dreams are worthy of becoming real. The universe is co-creating with you. Keep going.

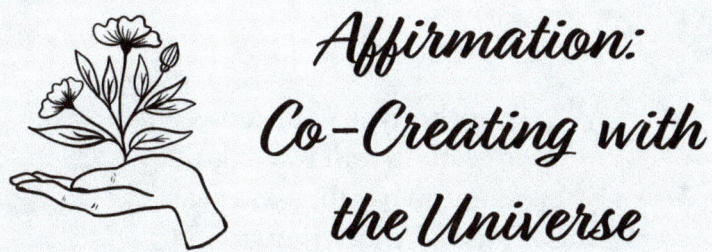

Affirmation: Co-Creating with the Universe

I trust in the magic of the universe.
I am a powerful co-creator, and
my dreams are becoming reality.

"Your body is your temple.
Listen to it, and it will guide
you to the healing you seek."
– Anonymous

Chapter 11
Healing through Intuitive Guidance

*I*magine being able to tune into your own body and discover the wisdom it holds – the gentle messages that guide you toward wellness and balance. Healing isn't just a matter of medical treatment; it's a holistic journey of understanding what your body, mind, and spirit need to thrive. Intuitive healing invites us to embrace our ability to listen deeply, allowing our inner voice to guide us to what brings harmony and health.

We all face challenges – physical, emotional, and spiritual – that can leave us feeling out of balance. But within each of us is the power to heal, to reconnect with our inner strength, and to restore harmony. Intuitive guidance, much like a trusted friend, helps us navigate the journey to wellness, offering insights that lead us to the practices, choices, and actions that support our highest good.

In this chapter, we will explore how you can harness your intuition to guide you in your healing process. From tuning into the subtle signals of your body to cultivating compassion for yourself, you'll learn how to use your intuition as a healing ally. Together, we will journey through practices, personal stories, and exercises designed to help you reconnect with your natural healing abilities and trust the guidance of your inner self.

The Art of Healing with Intuition

Healing is a multifaceted journey that takes shape in various ways. It may involve physical treatments, emotional release, spiritual reflection, or a combination of all three. Central to this journey is balance – listening to the signals from our body, heart, and mind, and letting our inner wisdom guide us. As we start to pay attention, we find that our intuition leads us toward the paths and practices that bring us back to harmony.

Healing can come in many forms: taking a rest day when our body craves it, finding the courage to express emotions that need release, or connecting with a spiritual practice that nurtures our soul. Each of these approaches is valid, and each of us will have a unique combination that resonates. No matter which tools or practices we use, it's important to return to a place of balance – one that honors the needs of the whole self.

Listening to Your Body's Wisdom

Our bodies constantly communicate with us. They express what they need, where they're carrying tension, and what might be causing imbalance. Often, we push through aches and pains or ignore signs of stress, but these signals are essential pieces of information that, when heeded, can guide us to better health and well-being. Many energy healing philosophies emphasize the importance of recognizing and understanding these signals as a pathway to healing.

Listening to the body means slowing down enough to notice the subtleties – an ache, a sense of fatigue, a flutter of excitement. Intuitive healing asks us to become quiet observers, to trust what the body is telling us, and to respond in ways that promote well-being.

Personal Story: Fear and the Back

Many years ago, when I made the decision to leave my stable 9-to-5 job to work full-time as a psychic medium, my body responded immediately. Within days of giving notice, I threw out my back, experiencing such intense pain that I could hardly stand or walk. My intuition told me that this was more than just a physical ailment; it was the physical manifestation of the fear I was feeling about leaving my secure job. The back, often associated with stability and support, was reflecting my uncertainty about my foundation. Interestingly, the injury also kept me out of the office in those final days, protecting me from an environment that had become toxic. This experience taught me the powerful connection between mind and body – and how our emotions can manifest physically.

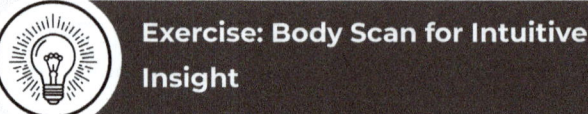

Exercise: Body Scan for Intuitive Insight

Purpose: To tune into the signals of your body, helping you become more attuned to areas of tension, discomfort, or emotion that may hold important messages for your healing journey.

Steps:

1. Find a quiet, comfortable space where you won't be disturbed. Close your eyes and take a few deep breaths to relax.

2. Starting from your toes, slowly scan up through each part of your body, noticing any areas of tension, discomfort, or sensation.

4. Pause when you reach an area that feels significant, and gently ask yourself: *What might this sensation be trying to tell me?*

6. Allow any thoughts, feelings, or images to arise without judgment.

8. After completing the body scan, take a moment to journal your insights. Reflect on what messages your body may be conveying and how you can apply them to your healing journey.

Emotional Intuition: Healing the Heart

The heart is not only the organ of physical vitality but also the center of our emotional world. We carry emotions – joy, grief, anger, love – within our hearts, and sometimes these emotions can weigh us down, creating a sense of heaviness or even physical discomfort. Recognizing and processing our emotions is a powerful step toward emotional healing, as has been taught in many spiritual traditions.

Emotional healing often requires allowing ourselves to feel deeply, without judgment or resistance. For many of us, this is a new practice. We've been conditioned to suppress strong feelings or to ignore the subtle signals our body sends when something is off. Over time, this can create a disconnect between our physical and emotional well-being. But healing begins the moment we pause, notice, and say: *It's safe to feel this.*

Letting emotions rise to the surface is not only natural, it's necessary. Whether we express ourselves through journaling, confide in a trusted friend or family member, or seek support from a professional counselor or therapist, what matters most is that we allow ourselves to be seen and heard. When we honor what we're feeling, we create space for healing.

The more we get in the habit of acknowledging our emotions as they arise, the less likely they are to manifest as physical discomfort or deeper imbalance. Our body is like a sacred compass. It lets us know when something needs attention. By listening early and often, we can care for ourselves in a proactive, loving way. In an intense moment, try to pause –

even briefly – and ask yourself: *Where do I feel this in my body?* *What is this feeling trying to show me?* These simple check-ins can help us become more present and respond with care.

Emotional intuition is about learning to trust that inner voice – the quiet nudge that says rest here, speak your truth, or *let this go*. It's a lifelong practice of tuning in, releasing what no longer serves, and returning to a space of inner peace. And in doing so, we offer love and grace to ourselves and to those around us.

Personal Story: Navigating Grief

After my mother's passing, I often felt a tightness in my chest – a physical manifestation of the grief I carried. Alongside this grief was an underlying anxiety, rooted in the loss of someone who had been my anchor. Acknowledging these feelings and allowing myself to truly feel them helped me find peace. Engaging in self-care activities – like going for nature walks, listening to music, and spending time with loved ones – also nurtured my healing. This process taught me that healing the heart involves both releasing emotions and embracing practices that bring comfort and joy.

The Power of Prayer for Healing

Prayer is one of the most powerful ways to bring healing to our hearts and souls. Many believe that prayer offers a direct line to God, to our angels, and to the higher forces that guide us. In moments of prayer, we are able to speak openly, expressing what may feel unspoken and inviting divine support. Often, answers come in gentle ways, like a feeling of peace or a soft whisper of encouragement.

Prayer doesn't need to be formal or perfect. You can speak aloud, journal, or even write a letter to Source – asking for healing, guidance, clarity, or whatever your soul longs for in the moment. What matters most is that it comes from the heart. In my own life, I keep a simple wooden box that I call my God Box. It's filled to the brim with handwritten prayers – requests for healing, support, and guidance for myself and others. Over the years, this little box has become something more. It holds not only my prayers but also my faith, my surrender, and my belief in miracles.

Time and time again, these prayers have been answered in beautiful and unexpected ways. Writing or speaking these prayers is a sacred act of letting go – of acknowledging what I cannot control and surrendering it to a higher power for healing, transformation, and blessings. In that act of surrender, I'm reminded to trust. Prayer teaches patience, renews hope, and strengthens faith.

A Prayer for Peace and Healing

In times of uncertainty, pain, or transition, sometimes the most powerful thing we can do is surrender – gently releasing what we cannot control and reconnecting with our inner strength. The Serenity Prayer has made a powerful impact in my own life. These simple words have helped me recognize and accept the things I cannot change, and to surrender to the love and grace of God. In doing so, I've often found that space opens for healing and even unexpected miracles to unfold.

The Serenity Prayer

God, grant me the serenity to accept
the things I cannot change,
Courage to change the things I can,
And wisdom to know the difference.

Let these words settle into your heart. Whether whispered in quiet reflection or written in a journal, this prayer can serve as a gentle guide whenever you feel overwhelmed, uncertain, or in need of grounding. Healing often begins not with doing, but with being – with allowing, trusting, and choosing grace in the moment.

Exercise: Loving-Kindness Meditation

Purpose: To cultivate compassion for yourself and others, creating space for emotional healing and inner peace.

This meditation invites you to focus on kindness and love, fostering a sense of connection and well-being. Find a quiet and comfortable space where you won't be disturbed. Close your eyes and take several deep breaths, letting your body relax with each exhale. Visualize a soft, warm light enveloping your heart, filling it with love and comfort. Silently repeat the phrases:

> "May I be well,
> may I be happy,
> may I be free from suffering."

Let these words settle into your heart, nurturing kindness and acceptance for yourself. After a few moments, expand this light outward, imagining it surrounding your loved ones, acquaintances, or even those with whom you feel tension. Repeat the phrases for them:

> "May you be well,
> may you be happy,
> may you be free from suffering."

When you're ready, gently bring your awareness back to the room and reflect on how this practice made you feel. Consider how you might bring more compassion into your daily life and journal any insights or emotions that arise.

Healing from the Spirit World

When we ask for healing, it's essential to stay open to receiving it. We can set an intention to receive healing at any moment – during meditation, prayer, or simply throughout the day. The Spirit world is eager to help us, often sending healing energy the moment we ask. When you sit in meditation or prayer, consider silently stating, "I am open to receiving healing energy from Spirit today." Trust that your request is heard and that healing will be given in divine timing.

Hands-on Healing

Each of us has the potential to be a channel for healing energy. You can use your hands to direct healing energy to parts of your own body that need it or to others in need. This practice, known as hands-on healing, has been used for centuries in various cultures. Try placing your hands on areas of discomfort – your heart, head, or any aching part of the body. With eyes closed, imagine a warm, gentle light flowing through your hands, soothing and healing the area. Trust that this energy is real and can bring comfort and relief.

Personal Story: Healing with a British Healer

When my youngest son was nearly two years old, his speech development was significantly delayed. While he had a few words, it was clear he wasn't meeting the typical milestones for expressive language, and as a parent, I couldn't help but worry. Through word of mouth, I learned about a renowned British healer and felt called to seek his help. During the session, I held my son on my lap as the healer gently placed his hands on him and then briefly on my shoulders. I felt a wave of warmth and calm radiating between us.

Within just a few weeks, I began noticing new words and a remarkable shift in his ability to express himself – his vocabulary blossomed, and he's been talking ever since. It was a moment of awe and deep gratitude, and it profoundly strengthened my belief in the power of healing energy.

Healing through Compassion

Self-compassion is often the missing piece in our healing journey. We tend to extend compassion to others but often forget to treat ourselves with the same kindness. Healing requires that we release self-judgment and offer ourselves patience and forgiveness. When we cultivate compassion for ourselves, we open the door to true, lasting healing. This concept is echoed in many healing practices that stress the importance of self-love and forgiveness.

Sometimes, this healing journey includes breaking patterns that have been passed down through generations. Whether it's a cycle of addiction, emotional neglect, abuse, or reactivity, we each have the ability to pause, reflect, and choose a different path. I've seen this transformation in so many clients – those who grew up in households filled with instability or trauma, and who, as adults, choose to parent with presence, communicate with compassion, or nurture healthier relationships with partners, friends, and even their own children.

For some, healing these long-standing wounds may also include working with a trusted therapist or counselor. Intuition can gently nudge us toward the right support system, reminding us that asking for help is a courageous and loving act.

Change begins with honesty and courage. It begins with acknowledging the truth of past hurts and deciding that those patterns do not have to continue. While it's not always easy, our soul can guide us in this direction and gently remind us that we are enough. It's okay to be different. It's okay to choose a new way forward. In my own life, I've had to make conscious choices to break free from limiting patterns and take responsibility for how I show up in the world. That personal accountability, while sometimes difficult, has been one of the greatest gifts – because with it comes freedom. The freedom to grow, to change, and to create something new.

Healing the self, in turn, becomes a gift we offer to future generations.

Exercise: Daily Healing Intentions

Purpose: To set a healing intention for your day, creating a roadmap that invites the universe to support your journey.

Steps:

1. Each morning, take a deep breath and silently say, "Today, I invite healing into my life. I am open to receiving peace, comfort, and well-being."

2. Repeat this affirmation throughout the day whenever you need a reminder of your commitment to healing.

3. Reflect on how setting this intention impacts your overall well-being. Write down any shifts you notice in your thoughts, emotions, or physical state.

The Journey of Healing

Healing isn't always a linear path. Some days are harder than others, and progress can be slow. The journey requires patience, faith, and sometimes an open heart to accept that not all healing looks the way we might imagine. Healing is about reconnecting with the wholeness within ourselves, forgiving the past, and nurturing a positive vision for the future.

Patience and Forgiveness

Healing often requires patience and, most importantly, forgiveness. Forgiveness helps us release old hurts and allows space for love to grow. When we forgive ourselves and others, we let go of burdens that hinder our growth. This act of release frees our minds and spirits, enabling us to live a life of greater peace and wellness.

I once worked with a client who had recently lost his partner to a sudden and unexpected heart attack. He came to me in heartbreak – grieving, searching for peace, and hoping for some kind of validation that his loved one was still near. His first session brought him comfort and a sense of connection, and not long after, he felt a quiet nudge – perhaps even from his partner in spirit – to continue exploring that bond. He signed up for a mediumship mentorship program, unsure of what to expect or where it would lead.

Over time, I watched this man open his heart in the face of profound loss. Despite his sadness, he allowed himself to be vulnerable. He asked hard questions, showed up with honesty, and let his soul slowly guide him forward. Four years later, though he still misses his partner deeply, he has rediscovered joy and connection. He found a spiritual community, formed new friendships, and even bought a motorcycle – taking long, meandering rides that offer him a sense of freedom and adventure, often feeling as though his partner is still riding alongside him.

Most remarkably, he discovered a new passion – one that has led him to helping others. In his spare time, he now gives back by offering mediumship readings to those who are grieving, creating space for healing and hope.

Grief never fully leaves us, but with patience and trust, healing can unfold in beautiful and unexpected ways. I've witnessed how, even in the face of profound loss, he found new meaning, purpose, and connection. His journey reminds us that while life may change, love endures – and when we open our hearts to healing and forgiveness, we create space for new beginnings to blossom.

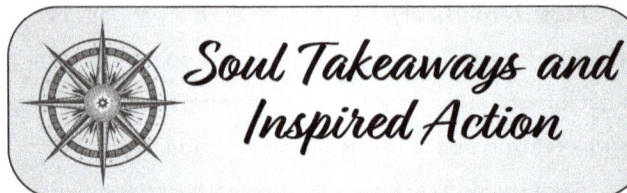

Soul Takeaways and Inspired Action

Healing begins with presence. It starts by slowing down enough to truly listen to your body, your emotions, and the quiet whispers of your soul. You don't need to have all the answers. Simply being willing to pause, to feel, and to allow healing to meet you where you are is more than enough.

Your body is more than a vessel; it is a wise and sacred messenger. Each sensation, each ache or flutter, carries a story and an invitation. When you respond with compassion and curiosity, you open the door to deep and lasting transformation.

True healing isn't about rushing to feel better. It's about reconnecting with your wholeness. It's about honoring your experiences, releasing what no longer serves, and gently reclaiming your strength, one breath at a time.

Grief, change, and emotional pain may ask you to slow down and sit in discomfort. But within that stillness, your intuition begins to stir. It guides you toward what soothes, what restores, and what brings light. Healing may not always look the way we expect, but it always knows the way.

You are not alone on this journey. Whether through prayer, energy work, the hands of a healer, or a quiet moment of self-kindness, support is always available. The universe, your loved ones in spirit, and the divine presence that walks beside you are always near.

Allow yourself to grow at your own pace. Give yourself permission to rewrite the story – one that includes rest, forgiveness, courage, and grace. You are not behind. You are becoming. And in that becoming, you are healing.

Keep listening. Keep trusting. Your healing is not a destination. It is a sacred path, and every step you take is a return to the truth of who you are.

Healing, like blooming, doesn't happen all at once. It unfolds petal by petal – quietly, courageously, and in its own time.

Timeless Wisdom

"There is a crack in everything. That's how the light gets in."
– Leonard Cohen

Healing reminds us that our broken places are not failures but openings. Through each crack, love and grace find their way in, transforming wounds into spaces of light, strength, and beauty.

"You yourself, as
much as anybody in
the entire universe,
deserve your love and
affection."
– Buddha

Chapter 12
Nurturing Your Intuitive Self:
The Power of Self-Care

ave you ever felt like your needs always come last? Imagine a life where your needs are honored – where taking care of yourself is not an afterthought but a priority that allows you to thrive. Self-care is an essential aspect of nurturing your intuition and supporting your overall well-being. By listening deeply to what your body, mind, and spirit need, you allow your inner guidance to flourish, creating a foundation for greater harmony and joy in your life.

Your body is often called a temple, a sacred vessel that carries you through this life. But your spirit, too, deserves reverence and care. When we tend to both – the physical and the spiritual – we create space for healing, clarity, and renewed vitality.

Self-care is not selfish; it is a loving act that allows you to be at your best for yourself and others. It's about recognizing when your energy is low, when your emotions need attention, or when your spirit craves connection. By treating yourself with the same kindness you extend to others, you honor your own divine light and strengthen your ability to hear your intuitive voice.

In this chapter, we will explore how self-care serves as a powerful act of intuitive nourishment. You will discover different forms of self-care – from physical activities to emotional and spiritual practices – that help you maintain a balanced state. We'll also dive into exercises that invite you to explore new ways to nurture yourself and connect with your inner wisdom. By prioritizing self-care, you're building a strong foundation for your overall well-being and allowing your intuition to thrive.

The Importance of Self-Care

Self-care means recognizing that your needs matter. It is about filling your own cup so that you have enough to share with others. When we neglect ourselves, we may feel depleted, disconnected, and overwhelmed. On the other hand, when we engage in acts of self-care, we cultivate a sense of inner peace and balance that supports us in every area of our lives.

Imagine trying to pour water from an empty pitcher. When we neglect ourselves, it's like trying to give to others without anything left to give. Self-care allows us to refill our pitcher so that we can better serve not only ourselves but also those around us. Whether it's physical, emotional, or spiritual care, tending to ourselves is essential to living a fulfilled life.

Self-care can be as simple as taking time to breathe deeply, resting when you're tired, or indulging in something that brings you joy. Listening to your body's needs and responding to them is one of the most intuitive things you can do. Just as your body and mind benefit from the physical act of self-care, your spirit also grows from practices that nourish your soul.

The act of self-care is, in itself, an exercise in listening to your intuition. When you make self-care a priority, you are tuning in to the messages your body, mind, and soul are giving you – messages that are often drowned out by the demands of everyday life. By making a commitment to nurture yourself, you're saying, "I am worthy of care and love." This, in turn, strengthens your inner guidance and helps you trust your intuitive voice more deeply.

Exercise: Daily Self-Care Commitment

• •

Purpose: To help you integrate self-care into your daily routine, ensuring you consistently nurture yourself and create balance.

Steps:

1. Each morning, ask yourself: *What do I need today to feel supported and balanced*? This could be a physical need like exercise or an emotional need like connecting with a friend.

2. Write down one act of self-care you will prioritize that day. Keep it simple, such as taking a walk, meditating, or spending time in nature.

3. At the end of the day, reflect on how fulfilling that self-care commitment made you feel. Did it help you feel more in tune with yourself? Did you notice changes in your energy or mood?

Daily Intuitive Self-Care Routine

To truly nurture your intuitive self, it's important to develop a daily self-care routine that keeps you connected to your inner wisdom. Below is a suggested routine that can help you integrate intuitive practices into your everyday life. Feel free to adapt this to suit your needs – intuition is deeply personal, and your self-care routine should reflect what resonates with you.

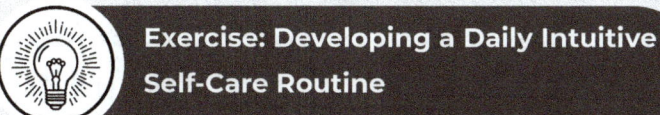

Exercise: Developing a Daily Intuitive Self-Care Routine

Purpose: To create a structured yet flexible routine that nurtures your body, mind, and spirit, enhancing your intuition and overall well-being.

Steps:

Morning Check-In:

- Start your day with stillness. Sit comfortably, close your eyes, and take three deep breaths.
- Ask: *What do I need today?* Let your intuition guide you and set an intention for the day.

Mindful Nourishment:

- Eat your meals mindfully, focusing on the colors, flavors, and textures.
- Trust your intuition to guide you toward nourishing choices.

Movement with Intuition:

- Engage in movement – yoga, stretching, or a nature walk. Let your body guide you to the type of movement it needs.

Midday Pause:

- Take five minutes to focus on your breathing, centering yourself and reconnecting with your intuition.

Evening Reflection:

- Reflect on the day by writing three things you're grateful for.
- Create a calming ritual, such as lighting a candle or meditating, to wind down.

Types of Meditation for Self-Care

Meditation is a powerful self-care tool that helps us reconnect with our inner selves and creates a sense of calm and clarity. While we explored meditation earlier in Chapter 2, which covered core principles, it is important to revisit the variety of meditation types available, as different practices resonate at different times in our lives. This section invites you to explore different forms of meditation that can support your emotional, physical, and spiritual well-being – each offering its own unique way to nourish your intuitive self.

* **Mindfulness Meditation**: This involves paying attention to the present moment without judgment. It's a simple yet effective way to tune in to your thoughts, feelings, and physical sensations as they arise, helping you develop awareness of your own needs. When you practice mindfulness, you are giving yourself the gift of presence. You're allowing yourself to be right here, right now, and that alone can be a deeply nourishing act of self-care. Even brief moments of mindfulness throughout the day – such as pausing before a meal, taking a few conscious breaths, or noticing your surroundings on a walk – can gently restore balance and bring you back into alignment with your center. With regular practice, mindfulness creates a spaciousness in your awareness, helping you make more thoughtful, intuitive choices throughout your day.

* **Guided Visualization**: In this type of meditation, you follow a guided journey to create a mental image of peace, healing, or growth. This is particularly useful when you

need comfort or wish to set a positive intention for yourself. Visualization can be a powerful tool for creating the reality you desire. By imagining yourself in a place of calm and tranquility, you are inviting those feelings into your current experience. These inner journeys often engage all of the senses – sight, sound, smell, touch – to make the experience feel real and immersive. You might visualize meeting a wise guide, walking through a healing forest, or standing in your future self's shoes. The beauty of guided visualization is that it allows you to explore new ways of being, feel supported from within, and reconnect with the energy of possibility.

✻ **Loving-Kindness Meditation**: Focused on cultivating compassion, this meditation practice involves sending loving thoughts to yourself, loved ones, and even those you find challenging. It can be an essential practice for emotional self-care. By extending love and kindness outward, you are also fostering a sense of inner peace. This practice reminds us that love is a limitless resource, and the more we share, the more we feel. You might begin by silently repeating: *May I show love to myself. May I be kind. May I release judgment. May I be gentle with my heart.* Let these words settle in your body like a soothing embrace. After spending time offering compassion inward, expand the practice outward. Send loving thoughts to someone you care about, then to someone neutral, and even to someone you find challenging. You might also offer these wishes to a situation that feels heavy or unresolved – surrounding it with light and the intention for peace. You could say: *May this situation unfold with clarity. May all involved be guided with compassion.* Love and kindness soften the edges around the heart and remind us that compassion is a strength – one that begins within and naturally extends to others and the world around us.

🕸 **Body Scan Meditation**: This type of meditation involves mentally scanning through each part of your body, observing sensations, tension, or discomfort. It's an intuitive way to practice self-care by listening to your body's signals and addressing them compassionately. A body scan allows you to connect with the physical vessel that carries you through life. By paying attention to areas of tension, you give yourself the opportunity to release what is no longer serving you. As noted in previous chapters, the body scan is a valuable tool for tuning in. You may recall working with it in Chapter 1 and again in Chapter 11, where we explored the healing wisdom of the body. This practice allows you to catch subtle cues before they become louder symptoms – a tight jaw from stress, a flutter in your chest, or fatigue behind your eyes. Bringing your awareness to these places with gentleness opens the door for healing.

🕸 **Breath Awareness Meditation**: Focusing on your breath is one of the simplest yet most powerful forms of meditation. It can help center you during times of stress and bring a sense of calm, particularly when you need a quick way to ground yourself. Your breath is a direct link to your life force, and by focusing on it, you bring yourself into alignment with the present moment. This meditation asks nothing of you except your attention. You might simply notice the rhythm of your inhale and exhale, gently lengthen the breath, or place your hand over your heart and feel its rise and fall. When your mind starts to wander – and it will – gently bring your awareness back to the breath. With each return, you strengthen your presence and build resilience. Breath awareness becomes a portable practice you can use anytime, anywhere.

These forms of meditation offer unique doorways into presence, clarity, and restoration. Depending on what you need, one may resonate more than another on any given day. Trust your intuition to guide you toward the practice that serves you best in the moment. With time and compassion, meditation becomes more than a technique – it becomes a way of being.

Personal Story: The Healing Power of a Walk

When life felt particularly overwhelming during a busy season of work, I began to take regular walks along a nearby beach. At first, I thought of these walks as a way to get exercise, but they quickly became something more. Walking beside the waves became a moving meditation – a way to clear my mind, breathe deeply, and reconnect with myself. With each step, I felt the tension of the day melt away as I listened to the rhythmic crash of the waves, the cry of the seagulls, and the gentle caress of the sea breeze. These walks became an act of self-care that not only nourished my body but also restored my spirit. They reminded me that healing often comes in the simplest of actions, and the act of caring for oneself is profoundly intuitive.

This experience taught me that self-care doesn't have to be elaborate or time-consuming or expensive. Sometimes, the simplest actions – like walking on the beach – can have the most profound impact on our well-being. It's about allowing yourself the time and space to just be, without any pressure or expectations.

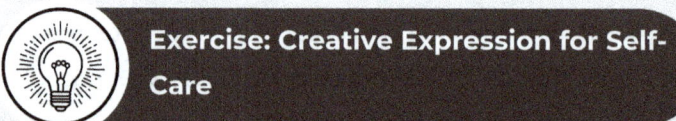

Exercise: Creative Expression for Self-Care

Purpose: To use creativity as a form of self-care, allowing your inner voice to be expressed and nurtured.

Steps:

1. Choose a creative activity that resonates with you, such as painting, drawing, writing poetry, or playing music.

2. Set aside 30 minutes to engage in this activity without expectations. Focus on the process rather than the outcome.

3. Observe how the activity makes you feel. Are you experiencing joy, release, or comfort? Let the creative process serve as a dialogue with your inner self.

Exercise: Nature Connection

Purpose: To help you experience the healing power of nature as an act of self-care, grounding your energy and nurturing your well-being.

Steps:

1. Find a natural setting – this could be a park, forest, beach, or your backyard.

2. Spend at least 20 minutes in nature. As you walk or sit, notice your surroundings – the sights, sounds, smells, and textures. Be fully present, releasing distractions.

3. If possible, remove your shoes and let your feet touch the earth, feeling the connection between your body and the ground.

4. Take deep breaths, allowing the natural energy to support and uplift you. Release stress or worries and simply be.

Self-Care for the Spirit

Self-care isn't only about tending to physical and emotional needs; it's also about nourishing our spiritual connection. Your spirit thrives when you feel connected to something greater – whether through prayer, meditation, creative expression, or time in nature. Honoring your spirit means creating space for intuitive practices and connecting with the energy that uplifts you.

Sometimes, spiritual self-care involves quiet reflection or journaling; other times, it may mean attending a community event that resonates with your beliefs. It's about finding what fills you with purpose and joy, and making time for it, knowing it nurtures your deepest self.

Personal Story: Painting and Peace

One of my favorite new forms of creative self-care is something wonderfully simple: paint-by-number. I'm not a trained painter, but I love the idea that – with a little guidance – I can still create something beautiful. Most evenings, after a full day of seeing clients and enjoying dinner with my family, I put on some classical music and settle in to paint. It's become a peaceful ritual, one that helps me unwind and reconnect with myself. On rainy weekends, my husband might be working on a puzzle while I paint quietly nearby – each of us nurturing ourselves in our own way. It's a reminder that creativity doesn't have to be perfect to be healing. Sometimes, it's just about giving yourself permission to slow down, enjoy the moment, and let beauty unfold.

The Journey of Self-Care

Self-care is an ongoing practice that changes and evolves as we do. Some days it may look like a long, restorative bath, while other days it's simply taking five minutes to breathe deeply between meetings. The key is to listen to your intuition and let it guide you to what will best nourish you in each moment. Trusting that your well-being matters allows you to show up more fully for yourself and for others.

Give Yourself Permission to Rest

Many of us have been conditioned to believe that in order to be successful, we must always be busy – checking off to-do lists, meeting expectations, and showing up for others before ourselves. But intuitive self-care begins with the quiet, powerful decision to give yourself permission to rest.

Rest isn't something that must be earned.

It's natural, healthy, and essential – especially during times of stress, change, or healing.

You are allowed to pause.

You are allowed to say no.

You are allowed to step away from the noise and come home to yourself.

It's okay to create space where nothing is expected of you – not even a plan. In those moments of stillness, your soul can breathe, your energy can renew, and your inner guidance can gently rise to the surface.

Affirmation:

I give myself permission to rest, to renew,
and to simply be at peace in this moment.

Self-care is an act of love – a love that starts within and ripples out to everyone around you. By nurturing yourself, you cultivate a deeper connection with your inner guidance, and in turn, you strengthen your ability to navigate life with grace, intuition, and resilience.

Self-care is a sacred act of remembering that you matter. It is not indulgent or optional – it is foundational to living a life that feels aligned, grounded, and intuitively guided. When you take time to care for your body, soothe your emotions, and nurture your spirit, you send a powerful message to yourself and to the universe: I am worthy of love, attention, and grace.

Listening to what you need and honoring it is one of the purest forms of intuition in action. Sometimes, self-care is quiet and still. Other times, it's movement, creativity, or connection. There is no one-size-fits-all approach. The key is to stay curious, stay kind, and let your inner knowing lead the way.

Your intuition is always speaking – through fatigue that asks for rest, joy that invites play, or discomfort that calls for change. When you respond with compassion, you build trust with yourself. That trust becomes the bedrock of your spiritual strength.

Let your self-care be simple and soul-nourishing. A walk in nature. A breath of fresh air. A page in your journal. A moment of prayer. These seemingly small choices ripple outward, creating space for clarity, healing, and deeper connection.

When you begin each day by asking: *What do I need?* and answering with love, you gently tend the sacred garden of your soul – nurturing it with each act of care.

Keep listening. Keep tending. Your well-being is not a destination; it is a devotion. And every act of care is a return to the truth that you are whole, worthy, and divinely supported.

"Faith is taking the first step even when you don't see the whole staircase."
– Martin Luther King Jr.

Chapter 13
Trusting the Journey:
Embracing the Unknown

I magine stepping forward into the unknown with unwavering trust, even when you cannot see the entire path ahead. Throughout this book, we've explored ways to awaken and trust your gift of intuition, guiding you toward a life of purpose, presence, and meaning. Many spiritual teachings remind us that the answers you seek are also seeking you, and your soul already knows the way. It's up to you to recognize and follow the signposts the universe places along your path. Think of your soul as your compass, always guiding you through life's ups and downs, helping you navigate the seasons of change.

Each of us is on a journey filled with twists, turns, and moments that challenge us to trust deeply. Even when you cannot see the destination clearly, there are always signs – subtle nudges and divine whispers – that show you that you're on the right path. This chapter is about embracing the magic of the unknown, following the guidance that presents itself, and trusting that every step you take is leading you exactly where you need to be.

Signs You're on the Right Track

How do you know you're moving in the right direction? Life often leaves us clues – subtle signs that confirm we're on our path. Just as trees know when to drop their leaves and flowers know when to bloom, your inner wisdom knows how to grow and evolve in harmony with life's flow. Trust that your timing is unique, and there's no need to compare your journey to anyone else's.

When you're in alignment, you might notice a certain ease, as if things are falling into place naturally. If you encounter challenges, they may still feel manageable, and solutions may appear in unexpected ways. At times, when things don't work out, this too can be a form of grace – a closed door can guide you toward something even better on the horizon. You may even receive literal signs – a bumper sticker that says "Right On" or a license plate that reads "Blessed" – just when you're contemplating your next steps. These nudges can be seen as the universe's way of answering our silent prayers for direction.

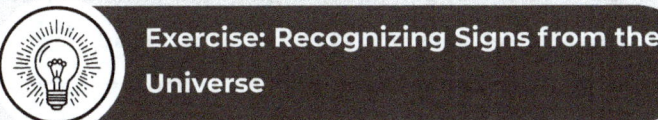

Exercise: Recognizing Signs from the Universe

Purpose: To help you become more aware of the signs and messages the universe sends as confirmation that you are on the right path.

Steps:

1. For the next week, make it a point to notice any signs that resonate with your current journey. These could be repeating numbers, song lyrics, symbols, or something a friend says that feels significant.

2. Record these signs in a journal, along with what was happening in your life at the time.

3. Reflect on the meaning of each sign. How did it make you feel? Did it help you gain clarity or affirmation about your direction?

By observing these signs, you deepen your trust in the guidance available to you and enhance your awareness of the universe's communication.

A Friend's Story: The Umbrella That Spoke Volumes

A dear friend once shared a fun challenge she received from one of her spiritual teachers. She was asked to choose a specific object – anything that came to mind – and see if it appeared in her life within the next 24, 48, or 72 hours. She chose a multi-colored umbrella. At the time, it seemed like an odd choice, but to her surprise, she began noticing them everywhere: in shop windows, on street signs, and even in a magazine ad.

What struck me most was what happened recently. My friend was in a quiet moment of reflection, thinking deeply about her business and what direction to take next. As she stepped outside for a walk, still holding that question in her heart, she looked up. On a bright, sunny day, she saw a family walking down the sidewalk carrying a colorful, multi-colored umbrella. It felt like a gentle sign from the universe, reminding her to keep going and trust that everything was unfolding as it should.

Following the Breadcrumbs

No one knows exactly where they're going – and if we did, the journey would lose its magic. Life is meant to be an adventure, with each experience teaching us more about who we are and what we're capable of. Following the small nudges – those inner whispers that say, *Let's try this* – can often lead to profound discoveries. Many have described these nudges as breadcrumbs, each one gently guiding you toward the next step. The key is to be open to saying yes, even when the path isn't fully clear. Saying yes to curiosity, to possibility, and to the unknown can open doors you never imagined and lead you exactly where you're meant to be.

Personal Story: Following My Own Breadcrumbs

Years ago, I was visiting Salem, Massachusetts, with my mother, wandering the cobblestone streets and exploring the city's whimsical shops, steeped in rich spiritual history. While she continued browsing, I sat outside on a bench, enjoying the sunshine and watching the people walk by. I was simply soaking in the energy of the moment when, suddenly, a deep knowing washed over me, and I heard a voice say, "It's time, Lori. You're meant to be a spiritual counselor." The message was clear and powerful, and I had no idea how profoundly it would change my life.

Soon after, I was guided to the First Spiritualist Church of Quincy, where I met my first teacher and spiritual mentor. I didn't fully understand where this path would lead, but I followed the breadcrumbs – classes, practice circles, and opportunities that began to open. This journey ultimately led me to embrace a new career as a spiritual psychic medium and teacher – one that has brought me immeasurable joy and fulfillment.

Looking back, I could never have imagined the places I would go or the incredible people I would meet. I am deeply grateful for each step of this journey and for all the opportunities to help others. None of us truly know where our journey will take us, but I'm glad I chose to trust and follow the whispers of my soul.

Exercise: Following the Breadcrumbs in Daily Life

Purpose: To encourage you to notice and follow the small intuitive nudges that can lead to meaningful moments on your journey.

Steps:

1. Spend a week tuning into the small nudges you feel in daily life. These may include subtle feelings to call someone, visit a new place, or try a different activity.

2. Each time you feel a pull toward something, jot it down in a journal.

3. At the end of the week, review your entries. Did any of these small steps lead to something meaningful? How did these moments help you feel more connected to your path?

This exercise builds trust in your inner guidance by encouraging you to act on intuitive whispers that often lead to valuable insights. If you didn't notice much, or you want to deepen your ability in this practice, continue the practice for another week.

A Soul Whisper on Trust

Sometimes the softest inner nudge carries the loudest truth. When was the last time you followed a whisper without knowing exactly why?

Take a quiet moment now to ask yourself:

Where in my life am I being invited to trust?

It might be a relationship, a decision, a transition, or simply the unfolding of your path.

Place a hand gently over your heart. Close your eyes.

And speak this affirmation aloud or in your mind:

"Even though I don't know how, I trust that it's all unfolding perfectly."

Let this be your reminder:

Your soul already knows the way.

All you need to do is listen.

Embracing Closed Doors

While intuition often leads us toward joyful, exciting opportunities, sometimes we encounter closed doors or obstacles. Many teachings suggest that these moments are often divine protection or redirection. Closed doors remind us that certain paths aren't meant for us, keeping us aligned with what truly serves our highest good. Sometimes, a "no" is simply a "not yet" or "not this path" – leaving you open to something more aligned or meaningful.

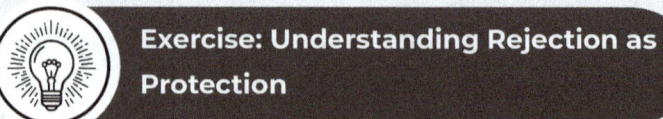

Exercise: Understanding Rejection as Protection

. . . .

Purpose: To help you reflect on past experiences where rejection or redirection ultimately led you to something better.

Steps:

1. Think of a time when a door closed, only to find that something better eventually came along. Write down the details of that experience.

2. Reflect on the blessings that came from this redirection. What did you learn from it? Did it help you grow in unexpected ways?

3. Write about how this experience influenced your life and what it taught you about trusting in divine timing.

By reflecting on past rejections as redirections, you can begin to trust the wisdom of closed doors and embrace life's twists and turns.

Personal Story: An Angel on My Path

Several years into my journey of mediumship, I studied with a teacher who challenged me to grow and stretch beyond my comfort zone. When the class ended, although there was an opportunity to continue, I felt a gentle nudge pulling me in a new direction. I was being called to join the ministry and pursue a path toward becoming a Spiritualist minister. Unfortunately, my schedule and finances wouldn't allow me to do both.

While it wasn't easy to step away, I sensed that the timing was purposeful. That chapter had come to a natural close, making space for something new to unfold. Soon after, I joined the ministry and found a new teacher and mentor who was kind, generous, and truly believed in me. She helped me grow in confidence, supported my development, and offered me opportunities to serve in greater capacities, helping me connect with more people in meaningful ways. She became an angel in my life, opening doors when I felt blocked and questioning what came next.

Though she has since passed, her light still guides and encourages me – and no doubt many others – as she touched countless lives with her love and passion for service. I am forever grateful for her belief in me and the kindness she showed. The redirection may have been unexpected, but it brought me exactly where I was meant to be.

Living in Harmony with Natural Law

Living in harmony with natural law means embracing universal principles like cause and effect, balance, and attraction. These laws are commonly recognized in various spiritual and metaphysical teachings as guiding us toward peace, purpose, and fulfillment. When we align our actions, thoughts, and intentions with loving kindness and integrity, we are more receptive to the flow of life.

Ways to Live in Harmony with Natural Law:

❋ **Cause and Effect**: Remember that what you put into the world will return to you. Every thought, word, and action has a ripple effect. Embrace kindness, positivity, and gratitude.

❋ **Balance**: Cultivate a balanced life, honoring both work and rest. Trust that your body and intuition will signal you when things are out of harmony.

❋ **Attraction**: Focus on positive intentions. Like attracts like, so align your thoughts with love and joy, and you'll attract experiences that reflect this energy.

By living in harmony with natural law, you create space for intuition to guide you toward greater joy and fulfillment.

Trusting What You Receive

Trusting your intuition takes practice and patience. It's a journey of building confidence in the guidance you receive. Even when you're unsure, learning to recognize and act on intuitive messages without judgment allows your trust to grow.

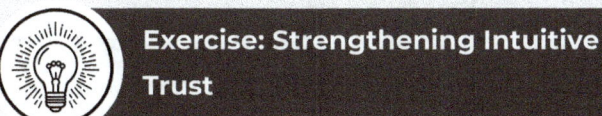

Exercise: Strengthening Intuitive Trust

Purpose: To help you develop greater trust in your intuitive messages by recognizing and acting on them.

Steps:

1. Each time you receive an intuitive nudge – such as a feeling to call a friend or take a different route – record the moment in a journal.

2. Act on these nudges whenever possible and note the outcomes.

3. Reflect on the results over time. Did your intuition lead to something positive? How did following these nudges make you feel?

4. The more you act on intuition, the stronger your trust in it becomes. This practice builds confidence in your intuitive abilities.

Affirmations for Trusting Intuition

Affirmations can reinforce trust and remind you of your inner strength. Here are a few to carry with you:

"I trust my inner voice and the guidance it brings."

"I am open to the signs and messages the universe shares with me."

"I am always supported on my journey."

"I am exactly where I need to be, and my path unfolds easily and effortlessly."

A Letter to My Future Self

Consider taking a quiet moment to write a letter to your future self. Let it come from the heart, filled with your hopes, dreams, and loving intentions for your journey ahead. Imagine your future self smiling back at you – strong, intuitive, and at peace. As you write, speak with kindness and encouragement, allowing yourself to feel the trust, joy, and confidence that are already beginning to blossom within you.

Share how you wish to feel – more connected, more courageous, more alive – and offer gentle reminders to trust your path. You might write, "I am proud of how far you've come," or "You are surrounded by love and guided every step of the way." Let your words be a blessing for the road ahead, planting seeds of faith and possibility.

When you finish, seal your letter and choose a date to open it in the future – perhaps one year from today. When the time comes, you may be amazed to see how much growth, healing, and intuition have unfolded. This simple act becomes a sacred promise to yourself – a reminder that you are always evolving, always becoming, and that the universe is walking this path with you.

Embracing Life's Journey: Trusting Each Step

As you move forward, remember that you are your own soul compass. Trust that every step, every sign, and every nudge is leading you forward, helping you grow and live authentically. Life will always present new experiences, challenges, and opportunities for growth. Embrace these moments, knowing that they're part of your unique journey.

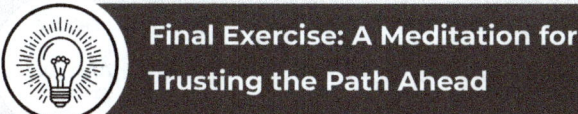

Final Exercise: A Meditation for Trusting the Path Ahead

Purpose: To cultivate a sense of trust and confidence in the journey ahead, allowing you to feel supported and guided as you navigate life's unknowns.

Find a quiet space and sit comfortably. Close your eyes and take a few deep breaths, letting go of any tension. Imagine yourself on a beautiful path in nature. As you walk, feel the support of the earth beneath you. Sense the presence of your guides walking alongside you. Notice how each step feels steady and sure. Reflect on the steps you've taken to reach this point and trust that the path ahead will unfold with clarity and purpose. When you're ready, open your eyes, carrying this sense of trust and support with you.

Soul Takeaways and Inspired Action

Your journey of intuition is an ever-evolving path. Trust that every choice, every moment of self-belief, and every nudge you follow builds a life lived with greater intention, presence, and meaning.

Throughout this book, you've seen that intuition is not just a fleeting feeling – it's a sacred connection to your soul, a way of living in harmony with the greater flow of the universe, and a quiet assurance that you are never truly alone.

Following your intuition often means stepping into the unknown, embracing the mystery with an open heart. It asks for courage – not the absence of fear, but the willingness to move forward even when the road ahead isn't fully clear. It's about noticing the signs along your path, trusting the timing of your life, and finding grace even in the unexpected twists and turns.

Every step you take deepens your relationship with your inner compass. Each time you say yes to a nudge, follow a breadcrumb, or reflect with compassion on a closed door, you strengthen your trust in the unseen currents guiding you forward.

This is the real magic – the unfolding of a life built on trust, faith, and the quiet bravery of listening within.

There will be seasons of doubt and times of questioning. That's part of the journey too. But even in those moments, your soul is whispering: *Keep going. You're exactly where you need to be.*

As you continue walking this path, let your intuition be your trusted companion. Let it remind you to pause, to listen, and to trust the wisdom unfolding within you.

You are co-creating your life with the universe – one step, one breath, one brave moment at a time.

The road ahead will not always be straight, but it will be beautiful. And it will be yours.

You are guided.

You are supported.

You are exactly where you need to be.

Keep trusting your journey. Your soul already knows the way.

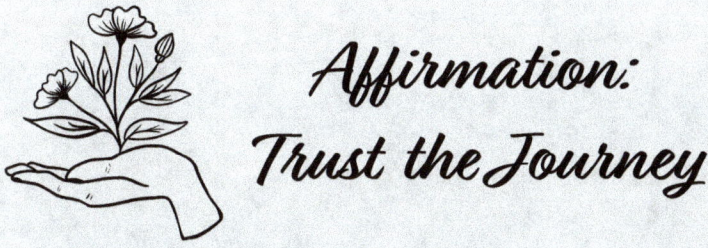

Affirmation: Trust the Journey

I walk forward with faith, even when I cannot see the whole path.
Each step is guided, each moment unfolding in perfect timing.
I trust my soul to lead me exactly where I am meant to be.

"Your soul is composing a magnificent symphony – a melody woven through every breath, every choice, and every step of trust. There are no wrong notes, only the unfolding dance between you and the universe. Trust the rhythm. Trust the becoming. Your soul's music is eternal, and it is beautiful."
– Lori Doupé Sheridan

"And the day came when the risk to remain tight in a bud was more painful than the risk it took to blossom."
– Anaïs Nin

Epilogue

$\mathcal{A}$s we close this journey together, I want to leave you with a final thought: your intuition is a profound gift – one that will continue to grow and evolve throughout your life. Each of us walks a unique path, and choosing to trust, listen, and grow not only helps us navigate life's challenges but also deepens our connection to ourselves, to others, and to the world around us.

Reflecting on my own life, I see the grace that has guided me at every turn. Growing up in a small town in Oregon, I never imagined I would one day be living on the East Coast of Massachusetts, surrounded by a beautiful family and doing the work I love as a psychic medium and teacher. I remember a pivotal moment – standing on the edge of a life-changing decision to leave a stable job and follow my calling full-time.

It was terrifying, and yet, an undeniable nudge reassured me I was on the right path.

My journey has been filled with unexpected detours, scenic moments, and even a few dead ends – each offering a lesson, each reminding me to trust my soul's compass.

There were times when I felt uncertain or unsure of my direction. But in those moments, I found the courage to change course, to begin again. Each leap of faith brought me closer to my true self. I think back to when I moved across the country, not knowing what awaited me – only that I had to follow the inner pull of my soul. That leap opened doors I never could have imagined, and led me to a life of service, connection, and deep fulfillment.

Throughout this book, we've explored the many ways your intuition can guide you – through the whispers of your inner voice, the love of those in spirit, and the synchronicities that remind you: *you are never alone*. These moments of connection offer light and reassurance, helping you feel supported no matter where you are on your path.

We began by opening your psychic toolbox, exploring the intuitive gifts and tools that live within you. These tools are not meant to be tucked away – they are meant to grow with you.

As you continue your journey, return to these tools with reverence. Building trust with your intuition is like tending a sacred relationship – it deepens over time through listening, reflection, and gentle practice. What lives within you is powerful. These tools simply help you remember.

Of course, mistakes have been part of my journey –
as they are for all of us. I've felt fear, taken wrong turns, and
questioned my path. But each time, I've been reminded to
trust the process. Even when I couldn't see the whole picture,
my soul compass was guiding me forward. I'm deeply grateful
for the guiding lights in my life – teachers, friends, family, and
Spirit – who reminded me of my purpose and the strength that
lies within all of us.

Take a moment to reflect on where you were when
you first opened this book. What have you discovered? What
practices or insights resonated most with your soul? Celebrate
how far you've come. And remember, this journey doesn't end
here. It continues every day, with every choice to trust, to tune
in, and to follow the wisdom within.

As you move forward, I wish you peace and joy. Know
that you can always trust yourself – even when the way ahead
feels unclear. Often, the greatest growth is born from the
unexpected. Your soul compass will always illuminate the way,
guiding you gently and lovingly to where you are meant to be.

Take every opportunity to serve, to connect, and to
live with authenticity. Whether through small acts of kindness,
offering a listening ear, or sharing your gifts, your presence
matters. Your light matters.

It has been an honor to walk this path with you, and
I hope these pages have reminded you of your inner wisdom
and the light that lives within you.

Just as we began by opening your psychic toolbox, I
hope you now feel your soul compass shining brightly, ready

to guide you forward. Trust that this compass will serve you through all of life's seasons – the celebrations, the challenges, and everything in between.

May you laugh, love, and live each day with joy – knowing your soul will always illuminate the path ahead. It is your trusted companion, your quiet guide, and your eternal friend.

Take that leap of faith. Trust in your power. Embrace every twist and turn as an invitation to deepen your connection to the wisdom within.

You are never alone. And every step you take brings you closer to the fullness of who you are meant to be.

Trust your inner compass.
Your soul will always guide you home.

"Knowledge is not
acquired for self, but
for service. It must be
shared so others may
also see the light."
– Silver Birch

References

Andrews, T. (1993). *Animal-Speak: The Spiritual & Magical Powers of Creatures Great and Small*. Llewellyn Publications.

Barnum, M. (2012). *The Book of Psychic Symbols: Interpreting Intuitive Messages*. Llewellyn Worldwide, Limited.

Berkowitz, R., Romaine, D. S. (2002). *The Complete Idiot's Guide to Communicating with Spirits*. Alpha Books.

Brennan, B. (1988). *Hands of Light: A Guide to Healing Through the Human Energy Field*. Bantam Books.

Bro, H. H., Agee, D., McGary, W. H., Carter, M. E. (1988). *Edgar Cayce on Dreams*. Grand Central Publishing.

Browne, S. (2004). *Sylvia Browne's Book of Angels*. Hay House.

Browne, S. (2003). *Visits from the Afterlife: The Truth About Hauntings, Spirits, and Reunions with Lost Loved Ones*. Dutton.

Byrne, R. (2008). *The Secret*. Simon & Schuster UK.

Cheung, T. (2019). *The Dream Dictionary from A to Z: The Ultimate A–Z to Interpret the Secrets of Your Dreams*. Harper Element.

Choquette, S. (2006). *Ask Your Guides: Connecting to Your Divine Support System*. Hay House.

Dyer, W. W. (2004). *The Power of Intention: Learning to Co-create Your World Your Way*. Hay House.

Eason, C. (2005). *The Art of the Pendulum: Simple Techniques to Help You Make Decisions, Find Lost Objects, and Channel Healing Energies*. Weiser Books.

Fraser, D. (2017). *Your Life in Color: Empowering Your Soul with the Energy of Color*. Hay House.

Freeman, J., Blotkamp, C. (1986). *The Spiritual in Art: Abstract Painting 1890-1985*. Abbeville Press.

Gawain, S. (1978). *Creative Visualization: Use the Power of Your Imagination to Create What You Want in Your Life*. New World Library.

Goldman, J. (2011). *The 7 Secrets of Sound Healing*. Hay House.

Gray, K. (2018). *Connecting with the Angels Made Easy: How to See, Hear and Feel Your Angels*. Hay House.

Greer, M. K. (2002). *Tarot for Your Self: A Workbook for Personal Transformation*. New Page Books.

Hay, L. (1984). *You Can Heal Your Life*. Hay House.

Hicks, E., & Hicks, J. (2006). *The Law of Attraction: The Basics of the Teachings of Abraham*. Hay House.

Hicks, E., & Hicks, J. (2004). *Ask and It Is Given: Learning to Manifest Your Desires*. Hay House.

Holland, J. (2018). *Bridging Two Realms: Learn to Communicate with Your Loved Ones on the Other-Side*. Hay House.

Javane, F., & Bunker, D. (1979). *Numerology and the Divine Triangle*. Whitford Press.

Jung, C. G. (1973). *Synchronicity: An Acausal Connecting Principle*. Princeton University Press.

Kabat-Zinn, J. (1994). *Wherever You Go, There You Are: Mindfulness Meditation in Everyday Life*. Hyperion.

Kabat-Zinn, J. (2013). *Full Catastrophe Living: Using the Wisdom of Your Body and Mind to Face Stress, Pain, and Illness*. Random House Publishing Group.

National Institutes of Health. (n.d.). *Benefits of Meditation*. Retrieved November 26, 2024, from https://www.nih.gov.

Neff, K. (2011). *Self-Compassion: The Proven Power of Being Kind to Yourself*. HarperCollins.

Newton, M. (1996). *Journey of Souls: Case Studies of Life Between Lives*. Llewellyn Publications.

Nohavec, J., Giesemann, S. (2011). *Where Two Worlds Meet*. Aventine Press.

Owens, E. (2005). *Spiritualism & Clairvoyance for Beginners: Simple Techniques to Develop Your Psychic Abilities*. Llewellyn Publications.

Phillips, D. (2005). *The Complete Book of Numerology.* Hay House.

Pollack, R. (2019). *Seventy-Eight Degrees of Wisdom: A Tarot Journey to Self-Awareness* (a New Edition of the Tarot Classic). Weiser Books.

Rand, W. L. (1991). *The Healing Touch: First and Second Degree Reiki.* Vision Publications.

Raven, H. (2006). *The Angel Bible: The Definitive Guide to Angel Wisdom.* Union Square Publishing.

Smith, G. (2004). *The Unbelievable Truth: A Medium's Guide to the Spirit World.* Hay House.

Soskin, J. (2002). *How Psychic are You? 76 Techniques to Boost Your Innate Power.* Penguin Books.

Stein, D. (2011). *Essential Psychic Healing: A Complete Guide to Healing Yourself, Healing Others, and Healing the Earth.* Clarkson Potter/Ten Speed.

Todeschi, K. J., Liaros, C. A. (2012). *Edgar Cayce on Auras & Colors: Learn to Understand Color and See Auras.* A.R.E. Press.

Van Praagh, J. (1997). *Talking to Heaven: A Medium's Message of Life After Death.* Dutton.

Van Praagh, J. (2009). *Unfinished Business: What the Dead Can Teach Us About Life.* HarperCollins.

Waggoner, R. (2008). *Lucid Dreaming: Gateway to the Inner Self.* Moment Point Press.

Appendix A
Glossary of Terms

> "Words are only stepping stones.
> Let them lead you back to what
> you already know within."
> – Ram Dass

The following glossary provides definitions of key terms used throughout this book. Whether you're new to these concepts or seeking a deeper understanding, this guide serves as a quick reference to enhance your intuitive journey.

Affirmation

A positive statement or phrase repeated to encourage a specific mindset or to manifest desired changes in one's life.

Ascended Masters

Highly evolved spiritual beings like Jesus, Mother Mary, and Kuan Yin, who are believed to guide humanity in spiritual growth, healing, and wisdom.

Aura

An energy field that surrounds living beings, reflecting their emotions, health, and spiritual essence. Auras are often described in colors that correlate with different emotions and traits.

Automatic Writing

A practice of channeling messages from the subconscious or Spirit world by writing without conscious thought, often used as a method to connect with intuition and Spirit guides.

Chakras

The seven major energy centers in the body, each associated with specific physical, emotional, and spiritual attributes.

Clairaudience

The intuitive ability to hear messages or sounds beyond ordinary hearing, often experienced as guidance from Spirit or one's inner voice.

Claircognizance

The intuitive ability to know information spontaneously without prior knowledge, often described as a sudden insight or inner knowing.

Clairsentience

The intuitive ability to feel or sense energy, emotions, and information beyond ordinary perception, often involving sensations or emotions related to others.

Clairvoyance

The intuitive ability to see beyond the physical realm, visualized as images, symbols, or flashes of insight.

Divination

The practice of tuning into guidance about future possibilities or gaining insights into the unknown through spiritual means, often using tools like tarot cards, pendulums, or runes.

Empath

A person with a heightened ability to sense and absorb the emotions or energy of others, often mentioned in the context of developing intuition and setting energetic boundaries.

Energy Healing

A holistic practice using energy work, such as Reiki or hands-on healing, to promote physical, emotional, and spiritual healing by balancing the body's energy.

Guardian Angels

Divine beings believed to protect and guide individuals throughout their lives, offering unconditional support, protection, and spiritual guidance.

Grounding

A practice to reconnect with the earth's energy, often through visualization, barefoot walking, or breathing exercises, to help balance and stabilize one's energy.

Guided Meditation

A meditation practice in which an individual follows verbal cues, leading to deep relaxation, visualization, or spiritual insights.

Intuition

The inner knowing or "gut feeling" that guides individuals in decision-making and perception beyond rational thought.

Intuitive Eating

A mindful approach to eating that emphasizes tuning into the body's cues for hunger, fullness, and nourishing foods, honoring the body's intuitive wisdom.

Intuitive Guidance

Inner wisdom or "gut feeling" that arises spontaneously, providing insight or direction, often experienced as a knowing without logical explanation.

Lucid Dreaming

The phenomenon of being aware that you are dreaming while still in the dream state, which may allow you to influence the dream's outcome and explore the subconscious.

Major Arcana

In tarot, the 22 cards that represent significant life themes and spiritual lessons, often seen as milestones in a journey of personal and spiritual growth.

Manifestation

The process of bringing desires or intentions into reality through focused thought, emotion, and aligned action, often guided by intuition and universal energy.

Mediumship

The ability to communicate with the Spirit world, allowing messages to be received from those who have passed on.

Mediumistic Channeling

Connecting with spirit beings or the Spirit world to receive messages, often used in the context of mediumship to connect with loved ones who have passed.

Minor Arcana

In tarot, the 56 cards that represent everyday experiences and situations, divided into four suits: Cups, Wands, Pentacles, and Swords.

Pendulum

A tool used for divination or accessing intuition, often made of crystal or metal, which responds to questions through movement.

Pendulum Dowsing

A divination method that uses a pendulum to answer questions by interpreting the direction of its movements, such as "yes," "no," or other responses.

Prophetic Dream

A dream that appears to foretell future events, often symbolic or directly related to the dreamer's life, providing insight into upcoming experiences.

Psychic

Someone with the ability to perceive or sense information beyond ordinary awareness, often through intuition or extrasensory perception.

Psychometry

The ability to receive information from an object by holding it and tuning into its energy or history.

Scrying

A form of divination that involves gazing into a reflective surface such as water, mirrors, or crystal balls to receive symbols and images for guidance.

Soul Compass

A metaphor for intuition as a guiding force, helping individuals navigate life's journey by tuning into their inner wisdom.

Source

The universal energy or divine presence from which all life originates. It represents the ultimate source of wisdom, clarity, and guidance, accessible through meditation and inner stillness.

Spirit Guides

Non-physical beings who offer guidance and wisdom, often believed to be spirits who have previously lived human lives, ancestors, or beings who have particular expertise to share.

Synchronicity

Meaningful coincidences that align with one's thoughts or life path, often perceived as messages or guidance from the universe.

The Fool's Journey

In tarot, the symbolic journey of personal and spiritual growth represented by the sequence of the Major Arcana, from innocence to fulfillment.

Third Eye

The sixth chakra associated with intuition, spiritual awareness, and inner vision, often activated through meditation or energy work.

Visitation Dream

A vivid and emotionally significant dream in which a loved one who has passed appears to offer comfort or a message, believed to be a direct form of connection from the other side.

Visualization

The practice of mentally creating images or scenarios to guide meditation, manifest desires, or clear energy. It is often used as a tool for connecting with intuition or setting intentions.

"You are not a human being
having a spiritual experience.
You are a spiritual being having a
human experience."
– Pierre Teilhard de Chardin

Explore these renowned centers and organizations offering opportunities to deepen your spiritual and intuitive development. Many provide both in-person and virtual workshops, making their teachings accessible wherever you are.

Spiritual Education & Mediumship

- ✴ **Arthur Findlay College (Stansted, UK):** A world-renowned college for psychic studies and mediumship, offering in-person and virtual classes, workshops, and spiritual education.

- ✴ **Lily Dale Assembly (Lily Dale, NY):** A community dedicated to spiritual development and mediumship, known for its summer programs and historic role in the Spiritualist movement. Offers both in-person and online classes and events.

- ✴ **The Journey Within Spiritualist Church (Pompton Lakes, NJ):** A Spiritualist National Union Church offering services, psychic and mediumship development classes, and community gatherings, both in-person and online.

Holistic & Personal Transformation

❀ **Kripalu Center for Yoga & Health (Stockbridge, MA):** Provides workshops on holistic wellness, yoga, meditation, and mindful living.

❀ **Omega Institute (Rhinebeck, NY):** Offers courses in meditation, energy healing, and spiritual growth, aiming to support holistic well-being and conscious living.

Grief & Healing Resources

❀ **Forever Family Foundation:** Provides support for families and individuals coping with loss, particularly those interested in afterlife research and mediumship.

❀ **Grief.com:** Features resources on grief and healing by David Kessler, focusing on understanding and coping with loss.

❀ **Hope Floats Healing & Wellness Center (Kingston, MA):** Offers grief and bereavement services, focusing on emotional support and personal growth through times of loss.

Spiritual Growth Centers

❀ **Circles of Wisdom (Methuen, MA):** A holistic center offering classes, workshops, and resources for spiritual growth and intuitive development, available both in-person and online.

❀ **Edgar Cayce's Association for Research and Enlightenment (A.R.E.) (Virginia Beach, VA):** Offers resources on holistic health, ancient mysteries, personal spirituality, and psychic development, inspired by Edgar Cayce's teachings. Provides both in-person and online events and programs.

About the Author

Lori Doupé Sheridan is a compassionate international psychic medium and spiritual teacher dedicated to helping others find peace, healing, and connection. Known for delivering clear, heartfelt messages from the Spirit world, she offers comfort to those seeking validation that love transcends physical life. Through private sessions, public  demonstrations, and workshops, Lori has touched countless lives, providing reassurance that love endures.

With nearly 20 years of experience, Lori answered a profound calling to explore her natural gifts, studying with renowned teachers, including at the esteemed Arthur Findlay College in England, an internationally respected center for psychic science and mediumship. Today, she empowers others to connect with their own intuition, reinforcing the belief that everyone possesses the ability for deeper understanding and insight.

As an ordained Spiritualist Minister with The Journey Within Church, Lori serves with purpose and compassion. She is also a certified medium with the Forever Family Foundation, a nonprofit dedicated to supporting the bereaved and advancing research into the afterlife and survival of consciousness. Lori has worked with clients around the world and has been featured on radio shows and podcasts, where she discusses mediumship, spirituality, and the value of living intuitively.

Lori resides with her family in Massachusetts. She finds joy in writing, spending time by the ocean, and creating lasting memories with loved ones. Her journey is one of growth and service, inspiring others to trust their path and to remember that the Spirit world is always near, offering guidance every step of the way.

www.LoriSheridanMedium.com

Continue the Journey

 ## Free Guided Meditations

As a thank-you for purchasing *Soul Compass*, enjoy a free bundle of guided meditations to support your soul's journey:

Sanctuary of the Soul
A peaceful, grounding meditation to help you reconnect with your inner sanctuary and the light within.

Meet Your Spirit Guides
A guided visualization to help you connect with the loving guides who walk beside you.

Download now:
www.LoriSheridanMedium.com/soulgift

 ## Soul Compass Wisdom Oracle

Inspired by the magic of *Soul Compass*, this intuitive oracle deck offers loving guidance to support your spiritual journey. Pull a card daily or whenever you need insight – your inner compass knows the way.

 ## Let's keep growing together.

Ready to go deeper? Explore Lori's upcoming classes, mentorships, and live events.

www.LoriSheridanMedium.com